Never Give Up, Son

Mario Guerra

Published in Australia by Sid Harta Publishers Pty Ltd,
ABN: 34 632 585 203
17 Coleman Parade, GLEN WAVERLEY VIC 3150 Australia
Telephone: +61 3 9560 9920, Facsimile: +61 3 9545 1742
E-mail: author@sidharta.com.au

First published in Australia 2020
This edition published 2020

Copyright © Mario Guerra 2020

Cover design, typesetting: WorkingType (www.workingtype.com.au)

The right of Mario Guerra to be identified as the Author of the Work has been asserted in accordance with the Copyright, Designs and Patents Act 1988.

The information, views, opinions and visuals expressed in this publication are solely those of the author and do not reflect those of the publisher. The publisher disclaims any liabilities or responsibilities whatsoever for any damages, libel or liabilities arising directly or indirectly from the contents of this publication.

The Author of this book accepts all responsibility for the contents and absolves any other person or persons involved in its production from any responsibility or liability where the contents are concerned.

All rights reserved. No part of this publication may be reproduced, stored in a retrieval system, or transmitted, in any form or by any means without the prior written permission of the publisher, nor be otherwise circulated in any form of binding or cover other than that in which it is published and without a similar condition being imposed on the subsequent purchaser.

Guerra, Mario
Never Give Up, Son
ISBN: 978-1-925707-22-9
pp326

About the Author

Mario Guerra was born in Griffith, NSW, on 14 April 1937 and lived in Beelbangera, NSW. After the loss of his father, his mother moved to Yenda, NSW, to be with her mother and father.

Mario spent his younger years in Yenda and at 18 moved to Lithgow, NSW, to join the railways as a fireman. When in Lithgow, he was called to do military service for three months and then citizens military service for a further two years. While in military service, he lived in Holsworthy, Griffith and Leeton. At Holsworthy, he took up the sport of boxing, which he never regretted.

He moved back to Yenda in 1957 where he continued to be a fireman. He had many career changes, from contract case maker, to fruit farmer, to truck driver, and town carrier in Griffith. During this time, he was an amateur and professional boxer and tournament promotor and played first grade rugby league for Yenda Blues. He became very good in both his chosen sports.

Mario lived in society's underbelly, amidst the type of things one has only seen on TV. His true story is a brutally raw account of migrant life from racism to mental illness and beyond. Mario has had a gun put to his head twice; once by a notorious mobster and the other by a man who had just been released from jail. He was taken down by three Mafia families.

His book is not one with a happy, fairytale ending. It is real. It is raw. It is written to depict his mother's strength, the cruelty she endured, and the way she forever shaped her son's character. The spectre of mental illness destroyed his family; his father, two uncles and grandfather collectively spending 140 years in mental asylums and his father's mysterious disappearance amidst cruel circumstances — circumstances that were never explained. The incarceration of his father, grandfather and two uncles point to a very different era in Australia's history.

My mother Caterina Guerra,

Introduction

It has taken some years to write this story. The time spent has been therapeutic for me. Through it all, my true friends offered their support. Professional people, my accountant and solicitor, were genuinely concerned. People still stop me in the street, some of them complete strangers, wishing me all the best. I have received letters of support from farmers I don't know as far away as Hillston, Hay and other areas. I received a nice letter from my cousin saying she wished she had the same close association with her mother as I had with mine. The letter went on to say that I should concentrate on the ones who love me: my wife and other six children. The letter said not to give up.

Perhaps this book may somehow help someone who has been told he/she is mentally ill. There is help out there from caring people. Names such as manic depression, bipolar disorder and schizophrenia are practically just that: only names.

Everything has not been written about the life and times of Caterina Guerra, her mother, and her son.

How do I finish a story I don't want to? There is much more to be written and said. By writing, I have hurt myself, but hopefully not my loved ones. My wife and our six children are my main consideration. Everything happens for a reason. The transport business I wanted to leave behind as a legacy for my children may not have been a good thing, as they probably would have incurred debts. As I continue toward the end of this chapter, I read somewhere that raising a family is the greatest career a mother can have. Spare a thought for the father. I am enjoying my new challenges and my new career. Up to now, I have enjoyed my wife and it has been a great joy watching our children grow.

Perhaps taking a wife younger than myself who gave me healthy children has kept me virile. The stress I have now is different. It is all about my children and my wife. I am sharing the same problems as other married couples with families.

I would like to thank:

Kerry Collison, SidHarta Publishers
Marie Pietersz, editor
Luke Harris, typesetter
Malcolm Wilmot, accountant
Darrren de Bortoli, De Bortoli Wines
Bill Calabria, Calabria Wines;

without whom this book may never have been published;

Suzanne Hopper, Presentations with Flair
Nino Gatto, for the loan of two photos
Daniel Johns, editor *Area News*, for allowing many
"blasts from the past" to be published
my wife Jacquie, for her assistance
our son, Walter, for his typing
our son, Justin, for the initial typing
our daughters, Jessica, Mary Anne and Katie, for their typing;

and to the people I have left out I offer my appreciation.

Some published extracts from local newspapers

During his 12 years of playing rugby league the local newspapers referred to Mario Guerra as "brilliant" and "sensational".

"Mario Guerra can score a try any time he feels like it ... mercurial, brilliant, Will-o-the-Wisp."
The Leeton Irrigator

"On his day, Guerra is the best player in the country."
The Daily Advertiser, Wagga Wagga

*This book is dedicated to my mother
who rose against almost incredible odds.*

She was to go above and beyond the call of duty in her efforts to save herself, her two sons, and, later her mother.

This is the true story of a peasant, migrant girl, born in a mud hut in one of the poorest parts of Calabria, Italy.

Caterina Agostino was born on the 8 June 1919, in Caolonia, Reggio, Calabria. In 1931, she came to Australia with her family on the Orient liner *Orana*. The journey took 40 days and landed in Melbourne on the 10 March 1931.

Not yet 16 years old, she was to marry my father, Paolo Lorenzo Guerra, at the Sacred Heart Church, Griffith, on 1 December 1934. By 26 March 1983, at the age of 18 years and pregnant with her second child, she was to lose her husband to the mental asylum.

Foreword

'Never give up, son, no matter what's ahead,' was told to me many times by my mother when I was about to become depressed. My mother also had to battle for her mind when I almost drowned and when my father was taken away. She would come back with, 'I won't give up.' When she was working on almost all the vegetable and fruit farms in Yenda, she sometimes didn't get paid. Other times, she worked for nearly nothing, with some farmers saying they could not afford to pay her much. She would say to me, 'Never mind son, things will get better.'

Caterina Guerra, in her lifetime, survived breast cancer, Crohn's Disease, ulcers, a hysterectomy, a stroke, a broken hip and high blood pressure. She never gave up and continued working at her beloved Griffith Base Hospital until she was 65 years and 7 months old.

A parish Catholic priest told me, 'Your mother is a saint.' Several times he said those words. He went on to say, 'Your mother suffered more than Jesus Christ.' Those kind words were taken out of context, perhaps, to reassure me of what a wonderful mother I had. Perhaps the reader must decide if I have been too presumptuous in adding these words to my mother's resume:

> *'To my mother's lifetime of disappointment, heartbreak and betrayal, of her great courage, her humour, and her mental strength.'*
> **Mario Guerra**

Contents

About the Author	iii
Introduction	vii
Thanks	xi
Some published extracts from local newspapers	xii
Foreword	1
My father walks to his doom	7
My mother has dogs set upon her	23
My mother's husband sneaks food to the hermit on the hill	27
My mother's sisters	31
My mother's brother, Giovanni, shot down by police	37
Racism	43
Bastardisation	51
Army duty	57
Back to football	65

Back to Yenda	85
A coal miner's daughter	87
Boxing	93
Terry Reagan	103
My mother's social life	111
Celebrities	115
Records	117
War and the Depression	119
In royal company	123
My first employment	127
I believe	135
Troubled times	147
Grandfather	149
When a girl marries	153
Big man from Vietnam in fight to the death	165
More about dad	177
Mussolini declares war on Italians	187
Giovanni and Natale Agostino taken out of the mental asylums	189
South American sting	195
My mother becomes very sick	201
A cure for cancer	223
Building of a transport empire	229
Kings Cross antics	235
Caught with our pants down	239

Razorback	243
The Griffith "Family" ties	261
Wrong move	277
True love	289
Wogs	307
The wheel turns	309

My father walks to his doom

My mother told me dad had a beautiful singing voice. She also told me dad wanted his son to be a doctor. According to mother, dad was a good worker and would take whatever work he could get.

The photos show a typical way of picking and loading grapes in the era of 1930s and 1940s.

One day he was picking grapes. They would use four-gallon kerosene cans with the tops cut out. This I know because mother and I picked grapes this way. The tops were dangerous, as the lid that had been cut out would remain jagged and after a while became rusty. It was one of these cans that struck my dad on his head, as they would throw them over the rows of grapes.

Kerosene cans and other types of cans would have their tops cut out and the jagged pieces that remained would be knocked down with a hammer, sometimes roughly. It was a tin or can such as this that struck my father, causing his head to become septic and giving him headaches. According to mother, dad did not bother much until several days later when his head had gone septic. With headaches that would not go away, he went to Griffith to seek help from the doctors. He walked there by himself, from Beelbangera to Griffith. Instead of going to hospital to get help, he walked to his doom, to a fate worse than dying — he was picked up by police in the main street of Griffith and taken to the doctor at the Griffith Base Hospital. The doctor could not understand what my father was saying and a second doctor was called in. My father was struggling with the language. The second doctor could not understand my father either and he was deemed insane. The document on the facing page is the actual police report and also the doctor's report.

My father was a strong man, as I've been told by some of his friends who are still alive today. According to mother's photos, he had plenty of friends. He apparently entered a three-mile obstacle course held at the Griffith Showground.

My father walks to his doom

LUNACY ACT OF 1898—FIFTH SCHEDULE.

Section 9.

Statement in connection with Patient.

[If any of the particulars in this Statement be not known, the fact is to be so stated.]

Name in full	Paolo Guerra
Age. (Give date of birth)	Born 10th August, 1905.
Married, single, or widowed	Married
Number of children living	One
Do ... deceased	Nil
Age of youngest child	11 months
Occupation	Farmer.
Native place. (Give country and town)	Braganze, North Italy.
Residence	Farm 289, Beelbangera, Griffith.
Religious persuasion	Roman Catholic.
Supposed cause of insanity	Not known
How long has the present attack lasted?	About 14 days.
Has he been insane before? If so, state the number of previous attacks, and the age (if known) at first attack.	No
Has he any insane relations?	No
Has he ever been an inmate of any institution for the insane?	No
Is he subject to fits?	No
Is he suicidal?	No
Is he dangerous to others?	Possibly. Has delusions that others are persecuting him.
Name and address of nearest relations or friends	
Special circumstances (if any) preventing the patient being examined before admission separately by two medical practitioners.	Nil.

(Signature) Thomas James Etho

(Address) Police Station, Griffith

[When the person signing the Statement is not the person who signs the Order for the admission of the Insane person, the following particulars concerning the person signing the Statement are to be added, viz.:—

Occupation (if any) ... Sergeant of Police

Place of abode ... Police Station, Griffith

adm 26/3/38   S 1410/15

LUNACY ACT OF 1898. THIRD SCHEDULE.

Order for Conveyance to an Hospital or Licensed House.

WE, the undersigned Justices, having called to our assistance Harold Skarratt Thomas and John Owen Walsh, Medical Practitioners, and having examined PAOLO GUERRA of Griffith, Farmer, hereinafter called the patient, who has been brought before us as being deemed to be insane, as also the said Medical Practitioners, and having made such inquiry relative to the said patient as we have deemed necessary, and being upon such examination with other evidence satisfied that the said patient is insane and was wandering at large

and that he is a proper person to be taken charge of and detained under care and treatment, do hereby direct you, Dr. SYLVESTER JOHN MINOGUE the Superintendent of the Hospital for the Insane at KENMORE to receive into the said Hospital the said patient.

GIVEN under our Hands and Seals at Griffith this twenty fourth day of March one thousand nine hundred and thirty eight

(Signature) _____ J.P.

(Signature) _____ J.P.

TO THE SUPERINTENDENT OF THE HOSPITAL FOR THE INSANE

Dad must have been about 32 years old, and his friends were about 18 years old. Whether he won the race is not known, but I am proud that dad, with his language problem, actually entered.

My father's friends and (inset) about to have a picnic on the Murrumbidgee River, Darlington Point

Some of my father's friends in the photos couldn't (or wouldn't) help him in his time of need. It is not for me to say they were lacking in courage, but I can only think this was the case.

My mother remembered most of them and told me their names. One married my mother's sister, another was the successful owner of a nursery in Griffith, the rest I believe mainly purchased farms in Griffith and became well-off.

My father holding two men on his shoulders

As the photo shows, my father must have been strong. All the men around him were his friends, not relatives. They did nothing to help my father, not bothering to help after he wrote to them and phoned them. Nothing was done to help dad. It was a tragedy.

When mother told me these things, I became upset. I would say things to mum, like, 'No wonder Italy lost the war. No wonder they put their hands up in surrender. They wouldn't help their mate who helped them.' Some people may think it is remiss of me to think this way. Perhaps we should move on, shouldn't we? But it was me who would watch my grandmother sobbing out the front of her house, saying to herself, *'Eo chu dise,'* (I told them, they did nothing).

It was I who watched her shedding tears while saying to me, '*Mi figiole non ficero niente,*' (My children did nothing). I remember going to grandmother and asking what the matter was. She gave me a smile, her face full of tears and said, '*Neiento figlio,*' (Nothing, son), and walked away.

I was 20 years old. My mother was very obedient to her mother. The stigma put on our families was cushioned by the great love I received from my grandmother, whilst mother was out working in the vegetable and fruit farms. The nuns were also good. We lived half a kilometre from where the nuns resided. They would come and visit us sometimes.

I enjoyed singing with my mother and grandmother around the fireplace in the kitchen. I was taught to sing as a toddler and until we left Yenda to come to Griffith, we would sing and laugh and joke. My grandmother always had a good story to tell the friends who would come and visit us, mostly migrant families.

Picking carrots, onions and parsnips with my mother and grandmother on our five-acre block, and going to the other farms and doing the same, made me feel secure. I had something to hold onto. I missed dad very much as I was growing up. Whilst I was working with mother, I would ask her questions such as, 'Why did they put dad away? Why wasn't something done? Why didn't anybody try to help? What about you, mum?'

My mother would try to convince me by saying the aunties had to get on with their own lives. They had to look after their husbands. The uncles didn't really want to do anything.

'Why?' I would ask.

'Well, son,' my mother would say, 'your father and your uncle shared a farm. However, they didn't get along. They had an argument, and your dad worked the farm himself. Dad also had a misunderstanding with another uncle, who was fond of the drink.'

However, my mother and my grandmother both said my dad was a placid man. The police records, the doctor's report and the mental hospital reports all said my dad was peaceful. Some of the other uncles, who achieved affluence, for whatever reason, did nothing. I was surprised, disappointed and hurt. My mother's sisters did nothing. I am sure they could have convinced their husbands to get him out of that place; he should never have gone into it in the first place. Not my dad and, it was to turn out later, not my mother's two brothers either.

On Monday, 10 February 2005, I met an acquaintance: a man I played football with. He said to me that morning, 'Mario, your mother was the hardest worker I've ever known.' However, this man and his wife lived in Binya, a dry area village about 30 kilometres from Yenda. Neither of them could have known mother that well. I would like to think that her reputation of not giving up, her bravery and her determination had seeped to Binya and beyond.

Also, I was speaking to a man that day who is in his eighties. He said he remembered my father was an extremely strong man. He told me he could lift a heavy metal wheel from the winery at Hanwood when others couldn't. He told me not all Italians wore white feathers. One Italian in the

1940s became a (Riverina) heavyweight champion; his name was Eno Cauduro. Another Italian Aussie traded blows with Hanley Tilden (nee Harry Hayes), one of Australia's great welterweight boxers. It was a street fight, I am told. The Aussie with the Italian name gave a good account of himself; his name, Tom Appolloni.

My father, Paul, committed to a mental asylum

My earliest recollection of life was my mother shooing a kangaroo out of her kitchen on Farm 1667, Beelbangera, with a broom. It would have been 1940.

But let us go back to the 24 March 1938, when my mother told my father to go to the hospital for a head injury. He had to walk from Beelbangera to Griffith, which is about 10 kilometres.

My mother was eight months pregnant and could not go, so it was decided dad would go by himself. Dad could not find the hospital and was found wandering around Griffith by the police. They took him to the doctor, but dad could not be understood and was deemed insane. The statement says my father had "delusions" someone was persecuting him, but this could have been his friend with whom he shared a farm. They couldn't get along, as my father was a hard worker. That friend of my father married my mother's sister, Theresa Agostino.

Page 13 of the statement said, "His present attack has lasted about fourteen days." According to my mother, the attacks were headaches after he was hit on the head with a rusty, aluminum grape bucket. My father's broken English was sufficient to explain to the doctors and the police that he had a son, where he was born and when, and also that he was Roman Catholic.

He also had a falling out with another one of my uncles from the Abruzzi region of Italy. My mother told me that her husband (Paul Guerra) was the first to ask if he could have a loan of my mother's mother for a month, to look after me while my mother went into hospital. He was refused. Some cousins told me their dad was a drunk. In that hard Depression era, I am told a lot of migrants hanged themselves, became alcoholics, went mad, or were sent to their homeland, Italy.

The other excuse was that whilst in the asylum, he

had escape tendencies. I ask the reader, 'Who would not want to escape from a mental asylum if they were sane?' I remembered mother receiving several letters saying dad had escaped, and I recall as an eight-year-old praying that he would make it. I would go to the far corner of Farm 737, Yenda, waiting for dad. I recall mother saving enough money to go to Kenmore Hospital at Goulburn, and then taking me by train to see my dad for the first time. I must have been about six years old. I remember watching my mother sitting on the seat with my dad, kissing him all over his face, hugging him and crying so much. I started crying myself, pleading with mum to take dad home. It wasn't that easy. Dad seemed oblivious to what was going on. I remember dad smoking a cigarette and calling my mother Caterina.

Because of our poverty, mother could only go with me when she could afford it. Italy was at war with Australia and relatives were not allowed to sign release papers to let dad out; or so I was told. My dad's Italian friends couldn't (or wouldn't) sign the release papers. With that act of cowardice, a family was successfully destroyed. It was a shocking thing that happened; it was a sin, a terrible sin. It should never have been allowed to go as far as it did. Dad was allowed to telephone some of his friends in Griffith to get him out, but they refused. According to my late mother, he wrote to them again and nothing was done.

My father's brother, Peter Guerra, worked in Koondrook, Victoria. He tried to get him out, and apparently the authorities said okay. They asked him how old his eldest child was and my uncle replied, 'Twelve years old.' It was deemed his six children were too young to have dad around. My mother asked several of dad's Italian friends to help, but they refused.

It was puzzling to be told my father's relatives were allowed to take him out, yet my mother's relatives weren't allowed to get their loved ones out.

Once he entered the mental asylum, my father would have been scared, and anxiety must have taken over. Perhaps they drugged him to keep him quiet. Once my father realised that no one was going to get him out — not his friends, not his brother, not his relations — he would have gone into a deep depression. That is the way we saw him when we visited.

My father (centre) and two friends, taken possibly in 1934.

My mother, being dirt poor, tried everything she knew to help him. I think mother must have thought a curse had been placed on us, as my father was the second of our family to go into the asylum, after my uncle, Natale. She must have wondered why her sisters and their husbands did not do more to help. Why did the police, the two doctors and the priest do what they did?

Forgive me, reader, for being a little cynical if I suggest it was just a job creation scheme, and they cared little about the misery and heartbreak engulfing my mother, grandmother and their children. It is my humble opinion that Father O'Dea has some explaining to do to God up there.

It was the same with the police; could they not have contacted my mother before they sent my father away? She could have pleaded to keep my father, given that she was pregnant at the time. My mother would have been barely 20 years old when the doctor and the police sent my father away.

My doctor today asked to be shown the transcripts, when we were speaking about the tragedy. The doctor, who had a lot of time for my mother, said, 'One of those doctors, who put your father away, could still be alive.' He was sad that the doctors of that era did not treat my father at the Griffith Hospital, where several days rest and some medicine were probably all that was needed.

I was not yet born when this tragedy occurred. As I grew older, I started to ask my mother more and more questions. In this instance, my mother's grandfather, grandmother and their family were at the Sacred Heart Church in Griffith, worshipping. My Uncle Natale would look at other people's mass books. The church people who sat next to him objected and complained to the parish priest, Father O'Dea, and my uncle was taken away to Kenmore Mental Hospital. There he remained until I got him out in 1988, much to the joy of my mother, and he resided in the Griffith Amity Nursing Home until he died at the age of 94. We noticed he always looked at number plates on buses or the family car when we picked him up for an outing or dinner, and he delighted in reading to us. He always seemed to carry the *La Fiamma* Italian magazine under his arm. Perhaps there lies the reason why my mother's brother was taken to an asylum: he just wanted to have a read.

A parish priest commits my mother's brother to a mental asylum

By the stance of the authorities and Father O'Dea's actions, a young man's life was taken away from him. Two thousand years earlier, Pontius Pilate washed his hands of Jesus Christ. Perhaps the good priest had to do the same to please his flock.

My late mother said to me that when my Uncle Natale was young, he went into a deep sleep for days. According to my grandmother, he never appeared to be the same after that big sleep. I have been told by residents in Griffith that a lot of people were committed to mental homes during the Depression era. Mother also told me that her father (my grandfather) lost patience with his son, Natale, for something and he locked him in the house they were living in and belted his son with a strap very badly. My mother, her sisters and my grandmother tried to get in, but they couldn't. Perhaps that also contributed to my Uncle Natale being slower in his mind. My grandmother refused to live with grandfather after that incident.

Shortly after this, my grandfather admitted himself into a mental hospital, where he stayed until I was 14 years old. Then, my mother, her youngest sister and I travelled to Orange by train and brought him home. I remember we were all crying with happiness. He stayed with mother, grandmother and myself for a while and then went to live with my mother's youngest sister and her husband until he became ill. He died at Griffith Base Hospital in 1952.

Father O'Dea

The first resident priest to come to Griffith was Father O'Dea. It has been said that Father O'Dea was impulsive, stubborn, and afraid of no one. He built a presbytery before the plans had been approved. He loved to have a good bare-knuckle fight, of which it is written that he had many. They must have been Protestants. However, my Uncle Natale was a Catholic and, sadly, the good priest hit my uncle first and asked questions later. Father O'Dea, of course, has been forgiven by all of us.

My mother, eight months pregnant with her second child, has dogs set upon her

The police would call around to mother's place once a month to pick her up and take her into town to purchase the groceries. This was the custom in the era of 1939. My mother asked the policeman if he could also take her to Hanwood on Murray Road to visit her older sister. She wanted to ask if she could have a loan of her mother to look after me for a month whilst she went to the hospital to have her second child. The policeman did, but my mother's sister's husband refused her request. He said her mother had to look after *his* children. My uncle was fond of the drink, had a fiery temper, and set the dogs upon my mother when she insisted. One can only imagine how frightened she must have been. Her husband was far away in a mental asylum; she was living by herself caring for me. My mother was eight months pregnant, being refused a loan of her mother, and having the dogs set upon her.

The policeman immediately arrested him and locked him up in the Griffith jail. My late mother told me that he too was on his way to the mental asylum, but for the constant pleading of his wife. I am told my aunt remained at the Griffith police station all day until the police relented and released him.

According to my mother, Raymond, my brother, was not born very strong. Perhaps the fright of those dogs had something to do with it. My brother perished five-and-a-half months after he was born. He died of pneumonia. Apparently, the great heat wave of January 1939 was too much for the infants and adults of that era. They were taken to the Griffith producers' cool room, and some survived, but 28 perished. I have spoken with the Griffith Ecumenical Society, spent time at the library, and visited the Griffith police to find whatever records I can about my father, my uncles and my grandfather. I have contacted Bloomfield Hospital in Orange, Kenmore Hospital in Goulburn, and

Ryde Psychiatric Centre, and also have spoken to some of their friends still alive from that era.

I have included cuttings of the *Area News* to assist the reader of this book to gain a closer understanding of my mother's courage and her determination to survive.

My mother and father on their wedding day, 1934

My mother's husband sneaks food to the hermit on the hill

There are many mysteries still to be uncovered about Griffith before the war and during the war. In the archives of Griffith, it is written that Paul Lorenzo Guerra, father of Mario Guerra, would sneak food and water to the hermit on the hill. Why sneak? Did the war have something to do with it? It was said by some that the hermit was a German spy; reason being he would wallpaper his rock walls with cuttings of newspapers about the war. Who knows?

The author of *The Hermit on the Hill*, said that Paul Lorenzo Guerra was probably the first person to find the hermit on the hill. This has been supported somewhat by the Griffith Genealogical and Historical Society.

It also said my late Uncle John, brother of my mother, stayed three months with the hermit on the hill. Much has been written about the hermit by another author. That same author knew dad. Because the war had just started, there was an instant dislike of Italians, even though they were invited to Australia to become new Australians.

During World War II, the hermit on the hill was interned as an enemy alien. It is said he was put to work building roads. However, after several months he was assessed, declared a deranged person, and moved to a mental institution in Orange, NSW. Six months later, he was released and sent back to Griffith. He brought back with him reports of another Griffith man who kept saying, 'Let me go home to Griffith; please, let me out.' That man could have been my father. Someone kind, possibly Doctor Burrell, had taken the hermit out. Sadly, my father did not have many Australian friends.

My dad was a Bersaglieri in the Italian army. They are one of the elite types of soldiers in Italy; perhaps that was the reason dad was taken away. A lot of Italians living in Australia wanted to fight the Germans, but it was not allowed. However, they were permitted to fight the Japanese.

Around the cenotaphs of Griffith and Yenda, there are Italian names of those who fought and died for Australia, their country. In Griffith, there are partisans still alive who fought the Germans.

What was done to my father, my mother's two brothers, and my mother's father should never have happened. When Donald Mackay disappeared in the 1970s, there was a public outcry across the nation, and also in many parts of the world. With dad, my two uncles and my grandfather, nothing was done. The apathy of those responsible was sickening. The doctors, the police, my mother's sisters, my mother sisters' husbands, and my father's friends may answer to God when that day comes. Evil flourishes when good men do nothing. I must also take the blame. The guilt upon my conscience never leaves me. Perhaps the suffering I saw living with my mother and grandmother affected me more than the others.

I was about 14 when my mother said, 'Mario let's go and see your father.'

I replied, 'What for? You won't get him out.'

The bullies had been teasing me at school. Also, some schoolgirls would laugh at me because of where my father was. I would go to church on Sunday mornings with my mother and grandmother and some of the Italian ladies would say, '*Dove le tue padre?*' (Where is your dad?). Then they'd give themselves a knowing wink. My mother would not go and help at the school tuck shop anymore because the Italian ladies would ask, 'Where's your husband?' with a smirk on their face. These rude questions they would ask my mother and me got all too much sometimes.

Another Italian boy would say, 'His father is mad; they are all mad!' Others would joke about my uncle who lived in Beelbangera and was shot down by police. I asked my uncles, I asked my aunties, I asked some of my cousins, if they could help me get my dad out. Most of them said the same thing: they are better off where they are. When some Calabrese friends visited my mother's eldest sister's place, they asked what had happened to her brother, her father and my father. She replied, '*Sono tutto pace,*' (They are all mad). I overheard this at the age of 11. I saw the look on the visitors' faces; the looks of disbelief that nothing was being done about these unfortunate human beings. These visitors didn't believe they were mad any more than I did, but the thinking of the day was that we, as cousins, would go mad one day.

I resisted this, saying, 'There's nothing wrong with any of them or us; they should be taken out!' However, no one seemed to care, apart from my mother, grandmother and me. I think the feeling was that Mario, his mother and his grandmother would have to look after themselves.

I was sorry for what I said to mother. Shortly afterwards, we visited dad who seemed so distant and lost. My Uncle Natale looked happy. Except for the grunting noises, there appeared not to be much wrong with him. My grandfather was happy to see us. I remember him giving us apples. All of us were crying. It was mother who said, 'Let's take him home.'

My mother's sisters

My grandmother and my mother's sisters

The photo shows my female relatives were attractive. My mother was called the *"piccolla bambola"*, (little doll). Note the way they looked after their hair. Their clothing was simple but nice. Their eldest sister, Anna, was living in Sydney at the time, and is not in the photo. Including my mother, all four of them married Italians from the northern part of Italy, from the Veneto region. The eldest married a man from the Abruzzi region, in the centre of the township called Ripa.

Three of my mother's sisters had good lives. Their husbands were good to them. Two of my mother's sisters became well-off, and the other was made happy by her husband, who worked on a grapefruit farm. The other two sisters had a hard life. One had seven children and a husband who was an alcoholic with a bad temper. I must say, however, when off the alcohol he was a kind man. He appeared to like or feel sorry for me. However, my eldest aunt (the one with seven children) seemed happy she had a husband, seven healthy children, a home, and a farm. She became a second mother to me.

The other sister was my mother, who had a terrible time — losing dad, losing her son, with no money, no work and hardly any food. My mother lost her breast milk, fretting for dad. Being alone was what caused it, according to my mother. Until my mother moved to Yenda, the two years spent without dad at Beelbangera must have been terrifying for her. A kind Calabrese lady told me she spent two weeks with mum when dad was put away. Whilst mother was preparing to have Raymond, the lady and her sister comforted mother at the farm. I find it very strange her sisters didn't visit mum much, but times were hard.

A comment mother got from one of her sisters about dad was, 'When they go like that, they have to be put away. Leave them there and forget about them.' Another comment from another sister: *'Vatinde to faciste tu letto,'* (Go away, you made your bed). The other sister was too young and she had to look after her father. Meanwhile, my mother's mother was staying with her eldest daughter, Anna, helping to look after her children. She refused to stay with her husband, not forgiving him for what he had done to her son, Natale.

My mother's second eldest sister was the one who looked after me for a month. She was married and took me to her house, something my mother was very grateful for. Mother made it up to her sister by working for 10 years picking fruit and vegetables on her farm. I remember my mother starting at seven in the morning and sometimes not coming home until seven at night. I would fret and go outside on that gravel road, looking for mum. Sometimes I would see her pushing her bike, as she often got punctures. My mother always seemed to come home very tired.

She normally would lie on her bed for a while with her overalls on. I was very disappointed my mother's sister and husband never went to see my father, or her father, let alone try to get them out of the mental asylum. My mother's second youngest sister achieved affluence through her husband's hard work. Meanwhile, my mother worked very hard for them, as did my grandmother and me. For many years, we picked apricots, plums, grapes, carrots, parsnips; whatever was on. It should be remembered my mother rode that bike for about 15 kilometres to work and 15 back. It was a rough road.

In the meantime, dad was vegetating with no one to visit him, although mother did when she could. I do remember one uncle going to visit dad at Goulburn when he was courting my youngest aunt. My mother, grandmother and I all made the trip by train. I must have been very young, about seven or eight years old. It was the second time I went to see dad.

I remember my grandfather was also at Kenmore in Goulburn. He would give us apples and seemed to be anything but insane. When I was about 12, I asked several of my uncles if they could help get my father out of the mental hospital. They all replied, 'They are better off where they are.'

My mother would tell me, 'They are giving your dad electric shocks to make him better,' and my hopes would rise again, but it wasn't to be. I would wait at the end of our block for dad to come home. I would pray; I prayed so hard to myself. I also prayed with my mother and grandmother. Throughout all this, my mother never lost her faith in God and nor did her mother.

I missed dad very much and needed a father figure. An uncle who married my mother's eldest sister would comfort me when I leaned on his shoulder. I remember travelling in a boxcar train on our way to Orange as a young boy, when mother was taking me to visit dad. A complete stranger was kind to my mother and me. I leaned on his shoulder for comfort and he put his arm around me. He seemed to know I needed a dad, even if it was only for a short time.

How different it was with my uncle back in Yenda! When seeking affection — I must have been about eleven or twelve — I leaned on his shoulder, only to be pushed away. I remember the angry look on his face as he waved me away.

I suppose he didn't know any better, leaving his mother and father in Italy and coming to a strange country. One of his first jobs when he came to Australia was as a horse breaker in Hay, a town about 200 kilometres north-west of Griffith. Back in Yenda, he was known as The Horse Beater. He was a hard man, tight-fisted with money and tough. He was to marry my mother's youngest sister when she was 15 years old.

I recall once my friend, Tony Dole, and I were picking grapes on contract for Mr Moretto. We were paid 1p a bucket. We were only kids, but we matched it with the contract pickers from Queensland. The contract price in that era was 20p a bucket. Being forever obedient to my mother, I remember becoming upset and crying, but not Tony. He let fly with a few choice words at Mr Moretto, calling him a mean *dago* bastard. My mother also became cross, saying to the boss, 'Come on, can't you do better?' And so, he did do better, by paying us an extra half-penny.

My mother's brother, Giovanni, shot down by police

It was May 1948, and I had turned 11. I can remember my Uncle John came to the house we were living in, saying he wanted to see his son. Looking back and thinking about it,

I think he also wanted to make up with his estranged wife, Marianna. I remember my uncle walking straight inside the house, saying he wanted to see his son.

An argument started between Marianna and him. I remember uncle slapping his wife. My mother told my uncle not to do that. He then slapped my mother. Another man, Don Moretto, said, 'Come on John, don't do that; do not hit the women.'

I will never forget what Uncle John said: 'What's it got to do with you, fella?' He pushed Don Moretto. Don Moretto stepped back and threw lots of punches at Giovanni Agostine. Uncle John got the worst of it. However, Don Moretto stopped chasing when John Agostino picked up an axe from the wood heap, about 20 yards from where the skirmish started.

Don Moretto went back to the front of the house where Marianna Agostino, her son, my mother Caterina, my grandmother, Don Moretto's wife, their son and I congregated. I ran to Uncle John crying, *'Zio zio,'* (Uncle, uncle). As I ran towards him, I knew he wouldn't hurt me. I knew he would have dropped the axe for me. My uncle was always kind to me. However, Don Moretto grabbed me and brought me back. In hindsight, what a pity. It could, perhaps, have saved another tragedy. My uncle was just standing there at the wood heap, holding the axe, not moving. It remains a tragedy that no one tried to talk my uncle into dropping the axe.

I am sure if his mother, or his sisters, his wife, or my mother had thought about it, they could have saved another dreadful tragedy. Instead, they agreed to call the police. Given that my uncle had problems with the police before, this was a mistake. Presumably, Don Moretto then went and called the police. Before long, the police from Yenda arrived. Sergeant Reeves and Constable Donoghue were their names. However, the *Area News* on Tuesday, 18 May 1948, stated Agostino went to the residence of Don Moretto and assaulted him. This is incorrect. He actually went to the residence of farm block 737 Yenda, where my grandmother, mother and I lived. The *Area News* also stated Don Moretto got another person to telephone the police. It is unclear to me whether it was Don Moretto or his wife who called the police. I remember Don Moretto walking away.

In the *Area News* it stated Giovanni Agostino menaced Sergeant Reeves and Constable Donoghue when they arrived to investigate the incident. Perhaps Giovanni Agostino would not drop the axe when told to by the police. I cannot recall (nor can any onlookers who are still alive) Giovanni Agostino menacing the police. He never moved from the wood heap. He was standing motionless, not raising the axe nor lowering it.

At about 11.00am (as stated in the *Area News*), Sergeant Campbell and Senior Constable Luxton arrived from Griffith. They immediately ordered Giovanni Agostino to put down the axe but Uncle John stood motionless and would not drop it. The sergeant repeated several times, 'Put down the axe, John.'

My uncle still wouldn't. The sergeant fired a shot into the ground near his feet. Uncle would not drop the axe.

'Drop the axe, John,' the sergeant said again, but John Agostino, son of my grandmother, wouldn't. The spectacle took place in full view of his mother, Maria Natalina Agostino, and his son, as well as the rest of us. The sergeant fired once more, this time hitting my uncle in the leg. I watched Giovanni Agostino flinch, but he still defiantly held onto the axe.

'Drop the axe, John,' the policemen said once again.

I thought, *This is it. The policeman is going to kill my uncle.*

'Drop the axe, John,' the sergeant said very loudly, but John Agostino would not. He stood motionless, holding the axe firmly in his hand. The sergeant shot him again in the other leg, but the brave John Agostino did not drop the axe. My Uncle John then turned and ran behind his mother's house. He ran into the carrot patch with the police in pursuit. About 50 yards into the carrot patch, Uncle John was surrounded by police. We heard the crack of gunfire once more, and we saw Uncle Giovanni Agostino drop to the ground in full view of his mother, his sisters, his children and his wife, Marianna.

Expecting my uncle to be dead, I watched with the other relatives, as Giovanni Agostino was taken by stretcher past his mother's house. His legs and his body seemed to be covered in blood. It was reported in Melbourne's *Truth* of the day: headlines said, "Police say he is mad, Doctors say he is sane."

I can't recall much more about what happened to my uncle, except being told he was taken to Morisett Hospital for the Insane. It is unclear how long my uncle was there for.

I do know of several cousins who visited him, telling me he was fine, but he would never come home. My uncle had been hurt deeply. He was expecting our relatives to do something, but it was not to be, and Uncle Giovanni was condemned to a life he did not deserve.

My mother's brother, Giovanni Agostino, seemingly left behind a legacy. His youngest grandson joined the police force and is currently a successful detective. It appears, in some way, Giovanni repaid with kindness something that was cruelly taken away for him, so many years ago.

Giovanni Agostino loved his family. He was responsible for getting them out of Calabria in Italy, bringing them to Griffith in Australia. He was to suffer a terrible fate.

Racism

August 1945, the war was over. I was eight years old. I was outside my mother's house and I had my Australian flag, waving it proudly, saying, 'We won the war, we won the war!' About the same time, there was a gentleman riding his pushbike on that road in front of our house. He remarked quite loudly, 'What are you waving that bloody flag for? You *dagoes* didn't win the war.' At the tender age of eight, I went into our hut and asked mother, 'Is it true we didn't win the war?'

The wisdom of my mother was there again. She replied, 'Well, we did win the war because we are Australian. We did win the war. But some people will say we didn't because we have an Italian name. Some people will swear at us. Others will spit on us, whilst others may try to hit us, but in the end everything will be alright.'

My mother's word of prophecy became true. It was my first taste of racism.

At about 10 years old, and I was allowed to go to town with my new bike I had paid for myself. I would pick carrots for my mother and she put the money away until I had enough to buy a bike. The local Yenda sergeant had three sons. I would play with them at the park in the heart of the town. There were others I would play with who went to the same Catholic school. However, a lot of my Italian friends were not allowed to go into town, as their parents were afraid they would be beaten up. I know several of my friends never quite recovered. They became timid, and are scared even to this day, but there were a lot who stood their ground. They were about eight years older than me.

On one instance we had climbed a willow tree about a quarter of a mile from where I lived on Barracks Road, when suddenly it was on. It was the O'Briens, the Conways and the Stevens, versus the Daminis, the Grossos and the Marins. There would have been about 10 on each side. My mate, Tony, and I watched from the safety of our tree. There were sticks, stones, eggs and plenty of fists.

'They are all crazy,' remarked Tony, who was later to become my best friend. After a while, everybody went home. They all appeared to have had enough.

When I was 12, my mother sent me into town for a haircut. Whilst I was having it in the barber shop, I noticed a crowd of about six or seven from the public school waiting outside for me. The ringleader said, 'Let's get that *dago*.'

I thought, *I'm in for it now*, but the kind barber let me out through the back door. I slipped away and lived to fight another day. Whenever my mother sent me to town for the groceries, the mail, the bread or the meat, I would always have my red bike close to me. It would nearly always be the same, being bullied by the mugs, the thugs, the would-be pugs; whatever they thought they were. I wondered if I would ever be brave enough, like the bigger boys, to stand up to them, or if I even wanted to. At this stage I was a good Catholic altar boy, trying to be what my mother wanted: singing in the choir, acting in school plays and eventually becoming a priest.

When I was about 13, it all changed. The Catholics were playing the publics. We were winning very easily. I was having a good game; I am sure it all started from there. Several days later, we went to the pictures at the Regent Theatre in Yenda with my mother and grandmother. We were watching the movies and I asked if I could sit with this man and his friends.

He replied, 'No.'

'I want to be your friend,' I said.

'You will never be my friend. I hate you. You are a black, *dago* bastard and you will always be hated.'

That was that, it did not worry me that much. I was getting used to it. However, when the movies finished, I kept getting pushed and shoved as we were walking down the aisle. He kept "chesting" me. I had enough and pushed him through the placards or punched him. Whatever it was, he looked silly with the placards broken all over him. That was that.

We kept walking to go home with my mother, grandmother, uncle and aunt when he came after me again.

This time it was in front of the Yenda producers' tin fence. I jumped on him and was having a good time. I remembered an uncle saying, 'Good on you, Mario.' They pulled me off him and he went home. About a week later, my mother sent me into town to pick up the mail at the post office. I was in there for not that long and, as I walked out, I was ambushed.

There was a circle of people. Some were grown up and there must have been about 15 of them. They were screaming and spitting and yelling, 'Get him, goof. Get the *dago*.' I was taken completely by surprise; the punch came out of nowhere and got me square on the chin. It didn't hurt me, but those screaming, spitting faces did. I wasn't going to win this one. I found a gap — my bike was close by — so I slipped off and lived to fight another day. Some Italian Australians would tell me that when they went to the Yenda Hotel for a drink, they sometimes had their beer spat into, or they were punched on the back of the neck. It was said some Italian shops were burnt down in the main street, Yenda. However, this was never proven and the culprits never caught.

There is a story told in Yenda about a young Aussie with an Italian name who was shot in the back with an air gun whilst home from school on the railway line. The wound could have been serious. When asked why they did it, one of the two people responsible, replied, 'My father was killing Italians over in Libya and I want to do the same in Yenda.' War is war and war is stupid.

As far as racism and bigotry went, Yenda had to be the worst town in Australia then. For Italians, it was certainly much worse than Griffith. I am quite certain racism had a lot to do with destroying my family. For example, when my father walked into the town for help, he was picked up by the police who said he was disoriented, which is another word for confused. He was taken to the hospital. My father could not make himself understood due to his poor knowledge of the English language, so they incarcerated him.

Another example is Sergeant Lyons, who shot down my uncle. He could have been more compassionate and talked my uncle into dropping the axe. That sergeant was to receive eight years in jail for taking bribes, according to my mother.

Another example comes from my grandfather, who was called "Lumpy Jaw" and was laughed and jeered at when he went into town with his horse and trailer. I can remember the big lump on the side of his jaw. My grandfather would go into town trying to sell his vegetables. It was his responsibility to feed five people.

Racism changed my life a great deal. At 15, I thought an escape for me would be to play rugby league, a passion of mine. We played at Weethalle in Group 17. I played reserve grade. In the game, I remember getting belted by big Reserve grade wheat lumpers. They seemed pretty old to me. After 20 minutes, a big lump of a man raced onto the field for Yenda and started giving it to those wheat lumpers. He was our coach. His name was Tiger Goring. After the game, he remarked, 'I wasn't going to let them belt you, son.'

Coming home, travelling by bus, I was called, "*dago*". I shaped up to him, though he was bigger and older. It was broken up before the fight started. However, for the rest of the trip the people in the bus remained strangely silent.

Perhaps the word had gone around in the bus that I was the son of a man in a lunatic asylum and they felt sorry for me, or perhaps the guy wasn't sure he could beat me anyhow. I think his name was Schifleet.

Years later I asked a former foe why they had given us such a hard time. He replied, 'We were taught to hate, Mario; we didn't know any better.'

In 1950, we would ride our bikes to a farm in Yenda. There was myself (an Italian), an aboriginal, two Greeks and three Australians picking carrots for the Sicilian new Australian farmer. We all got on very well. It brings to mind something my mother told me during her many years working at Griffith Base Hospital.

'I'm sorry, son,' she said. I asked, 'What for,' and she replied, 'For being such a peasant. I didn't have enough education.'

I do recall saying there was nothing to be sorry for. I often wonder what my mother meant.

In 1954, I was 17 and wanted to try again. I went to the Scout Hall where the footballers trained. Yenda was now in Group 20. I looked through the window and recognised a lot of the men. They were the same blokes that surrounded and spat on me several years ago at the Yenda Post Office.

I went home despairing of ever getting to play rugby league. My mother could not find work, nor could my grandmother. At the time, I had a good job that I thoroughly enjoyed: making fruit boxes on contract. I became fast. I would earn up to £40 a week. That was a lot of money at the time. I started work at the age of 14. I was still there at

18 and making good money. I was helping support mother and grandmother.

The hours were long. During the busy season, we would work seven days a week up to 12 hours a day, then come back at night and work a couple more hours. My hands would get calloused; sometimes I would belt my thumb and my fingers. Many times, I hit my thumb and fingers with the case-making hammer. I was happy with the job and happy living in that two-room hut with my mother and grandmother. We had a fireplace and grandmother would sing us songs. My mother and I would join in. Friends, relatives and neighbours would visit us, and in turn we would visit our friends, neighbours and relatives.

Our neighbours nearest us were very kind. Their children were like brother and sister to me, and their parents became my godfather and godmother. We were confirmed within the Catholic Church, where we promised not to drink alcohol. However, the party was held at my godfather's place and at the age of 12, I broke my first promise by drinking lots of alcohol with my mates.

It was different now than to a decade earlier, with my mother living in loneliness and sadness. We were very poor and the void of missing dad never left us. Mother knew (but couldn't tell me) that dad was never going to come back. It was unfair of me to continually ask my mother to get my dad out. Mother would try to explain, 'Mario, if I were able to get your father out of the mental hospital, he would run away; he would be an extra burden and an extra mouth to feed.'

My mother, of course, was right.

Bastardisation

Before I left to go to Lithgow, whilst working at my job making wooden boxes, I was attacked by four men working there. They straddled me across the roller where the fruit boxes (mainly oranges) would roll along after the boxes were packed. I pleaded with them, I begged them; I called out to the boss, who turned his head the other way. They took off my clothes and attempted to push half an orange into my backside then they turned me around and interfered with my private parts. My shame and indignity cried out for revenge.

When they had finished, I said to them, 'Upon the grave of my father, I will get you all. I am going away, but I will make things even when I come back.' My father, of course, was not dead at that stage, but it stopped people from asking questions. Why did these four men do what they did? I can think of only one reason: I could make boxes fast, very fast, and I was quicker than them and as I was sometimes earning twice the money they could, they were jealous.

After the assault, I rode my bike home. Mum could see I was distressed. She had just come home from working in the vegetable paddocks. She finally got it out of me; I was just so upset. My mother became very angry. She first rode her bike to the police station in Yenda and complained to Constable Bugde. He tried to laugh it off, telling my mother not to worry about it. My mother could tell he was friends with those people, so she proceeded to ride her bike to Griffith Police Station.

Can the reader imagine? My mother was going to Griffith to see that justice was done, yet the trip was 20 kilometres past the Yenda Bridge. Mother received a puncture, a common occurrence in those days, and she had to push her bike home. She repaired the puncture, got on her bike again, and went and made her complaint to one of the two bosses who lived about four kilometres away from Barracks Road. Mother came back and the boss said he would look into it. Mother was disappointed. She knew the boss wanted it hushed up, plus there was business to think of.

Before I went away to Lithgow, I thought Yenda was a horrible place to live: being called a black *dago*, black bastard, greasy *wog*, *spag* gang, the garlic eater. Being asked questions, *'Dove el tu padre?'* or *'Tu padre e' paco'* (Where is your dad? Your dad is mad). Mother seemed to be always working in those vegetable paddocks. My grandmother was deaf and could not speak a word of English. She was a lovable, dear, kind, old lady seeing her own daughter suffer with the loss of her own husband and son. She had to watch my mother work so hard to support them both.

Through my youth and into my late teenage years, I remember mother struggling on the five-acre block of land. The agreement was that the two uncles or our kind neighbour would prepare the land by grading, disking, making the furrows and sowing the vegetables, whilst my mother and grandmother would give their labour. This involved picking and weighing of peas, carrots, parsnips, onions, beetroot, rock melons, cauliflowers and cabbages. I remember, one year, mother planting tomatoes for the cannery.

It used to be mostly carrots that were grown. My mother would clean out the grass growing in the furrows with a horse and what was called a "scarifier". After the carrots were picked, they would be put into hessian bags and then she would throw them onto the horse and trailer. My mother was assisted by me and the uncles when they could. The bags of carrots would then be taken to the front of our hut, where grandad had built a dam, and the carrots would be left to soak in the dam overnight. Very early the next morning, my mother would break the ice on the dam and start to wash the dirt off the carrots by holding the hessian bags on each side and shaking the bag. It was back-breaking work. The bags would then be thrown onto the trailer, tipped into a 112lb bag (960 kilos), sewn up with a needle and twine, and taken to the train at the Yenda producers ready for their voyage to the Sydney markets.

The produce would not arrive at the Sydney markets until the following morning, Because of the almost two-day journey, sometimes the produce became unsaleable. I remember once mother received payment of 2½p and sometimes she would receive a bill. Where my mother got her strength to weed the grass out of those vegetables, week in and week out, for months and years, in the boiling sun, is beyond understanding. My grandmother and I would work alongside her. By 2.00pm, the sun in summer could get really hot and at times it seemed she would faint. Even the uncle told her she should rest. It has been said Italians work too hard, and I agree. Perhaps my mother wanted to make sure her job was safe.

I could not match my mother's determination to stay in that boiling sun and would seek shade under a tree. I can remember, to this day, my mother, under that hot sun, drinking water out of the hessian bag and giving a sigh of relief. The farmer's wife, who was my mother's sister, would bring us morning and afternoon tea, which was a welcome respite, but not enough to stop my dislike of vegetable farming.

I think this dislike started when watching my mother working so hard. On occasions, she would drink water from the hessian bag. When she finished drinking, she would immediately go back to hoeing weeds from the growing vegetables. In an almost slave-like fashion, she stubbornly refused to give up and take a rest from that sun. I would have been about 14 or 15 years old.

We lived in poverty. The toilet was a bucket, which would be carried by my mother and grandmother to be emptied. When I grew older, it was then done by me. We had two goats; we would take turns to milk them. From a very early age, we would pick milk thistles from the side of the road. I remember my mother's youngest sister also picking thistles on the side of the road. She wasn't married and was living with us. They would boil the milk thistles and we would eat the thistles then drink up the soup, or my mother and grandmother would make a salad out of the thistles. I can also remember from the age three to the age of 12, living in that two-room hut, which was always spotless. We had one luxury in that era and that was having wooden floors that were varnished. We had a ladder in my mother's house, which went up to the attic. That's where I slept.

My mother, grandmother and my mother's sister all slept downstairs. The next room was the kitchen. The two rooms were quite large; grandfather must have known what he was doing. We would wash ourselves outside where grandfather had provided a small channel and we had a tub. Underneath the attic was the stable, where the horses and the goats were kept. The stable was not only our bathroom, but also a place to keep the food cool. Mother and grandmother would dig a hole in the ground. That's the way things would stay fresh in those days.

Army duty

On 11 May 1956, I was called to do national service with the 19th Battalion, Holsworthy. I was with Dog Company. I was stoked, first beautiful Lithgow, now the

army! Had I stayed in Yenda, I would not have received this call, as not one person in my age group there received a call-up from the army. I immediately took up boxing with one thing on my mind: get the so-and-so bastards who made my life so miserable back in Yenda. First, I had to be good enough to represent Dog Company. I won my first two bouts easily, then I represented Dog Company against Easy Company. I won that too in the first round. My next two bouts against Baker Company and Able Company were easy, all I had to do was walk across the ring to my opponent's side and claim what was called a walkover win, as the opponent was on the outside of the ring looking in, not wishing to fight. I was then to fight Johnny McMannus. He was from Charlie Company. The winner would be matched against the best from the 13th Battalion from the Regular Army.

The night before the fight I went to bed early. I was extremely confident, when this fellow we called Two Up, because of his gambling habits, came into the barracks. Two Up was representing Charlie Company in the lightweight division, I was in the welterweight class.

'Come on, Mario, let's go out to Liverpool and have a good time.'

I replied, 'Can't do it, Two Up, I have a big fight tomorrow,' but Two Up was persistent.

'Look, I know for a fact that he's not going to turn up. He's scared of you, 'You will get another walkover win.' Two Up said to me.

'What about you?' I said.

'Why don't you have a good sleep?'

'Oh, I will beat him easy.

Come on, let's go.'

Two Up kept at me.

I threatened Two Up and told him I would punch him if he didn't go away.

But he kept at me. I pushed him out of the barracks door and locked it. He kept at me from outside, 'Come on, let's go.' Then Two Up came in through one of the open windows.

I should have realised there was more to this, but instead I laughed and said, 'Let's go.' Because it was out of bounds, we sneaked out through what was called "nut and bolt camp", (the new Australian migrants). A lot were from the Baltic State, hence the nickname "nut and bolt". They were housed at Villawood. Two Up knew it all; we must have tried every beer in every hotel in Liverpool, ran away from every police provost there was, and chased every woman. Two Up kept plying the beer into me and I kept drinking it. I was so sick, I still remember to this day vomiting everywhere and wanting to go to sleep, but Two Up wouldn't let me. How we got home, I don't remember. I remember I went to the barracks and slept for about two hours. It was then 6.00am; time to get up for *reveille* roll call, then breakfast. I didn't have to do anything else except wait my turn to fight.

It was my hardest fight ever. It was held in the open air at Holsworthy Army Barracks against Johnny McMannus. The tournament started at 2.00pm, under a hot sun. For some reason, they had the lights on as well. I can't ever recall being as sick as I was that day, and I'm sure Johnny McMannus knew I was not fit.

Two Up fought before me; he lost. My turn came, and I knew I had to knock him out in the first round if I was to win. I started fast and knocked down Johnny McMannus for an eight-count, but he got up. I had him wobbly a couple of times, but he was a good fighter and he lasted the round. We came out for the second round and it was me kissing canvas after an eight-count. I got up, but Johnny was more experienced than me; he kept turning me into the ropes. As we prepared for the third and final round, my trainer told me, 'Stop eating his left lead, go underneath it and cross over with your right.' That I did, and I had Johnny wobbly again. It was the toughest fight I can ever recall, and it taught me a lesson.

I knew I lost that fight by a close decision. I received a black eye as well. I was picked in the squad for training in case someone withdrew. They didn't and Johnny McMannus went on to win two fights against the Regular Army.

Mario Guerra and Johnny McMannus

A highlight of my foray into boxing was when we went training in Snowy Robbin's gymnasium, at Erskineville. I watched the great Darby Brown train for his upcoming fight with George Barnes for the Empire title, which he won. While I was there, I had many sparring sessions with others and caught the eye of Bernie Halls, a former great boxer and also one of Australia's leading trainers at the time. He approached me saying I could be a good fighter and would go a long way. It was my chance, but I didn't take it, saying I would let him know: there was my mother and grandmother to think of, there was a girl waiting for me in Lithgow, and there was my father rotting away in a mental asylum. Was it my shame about our family's mental illness, or was it that I had lost confidence after losing on a points decision to Johnny McMannus?

I was 19 years old and in the arms of my girlfriend. I found comfort there for a while, but dad's face was always there. There was not a day went by that I did not think of dad.

It was now August 1957. My mother wanted me to come home. She had found a job working at Griffith District Hospital and she wanted me to come back home and look after grandmother. I had been dreading this moment. I knew I had to return home, because blood is blood, family is family. It was my mother and grandmother versus my girlfriend. I told my girlfriend I could not marry her; I could not marry her anymore because my father was mad and I was probably going the same way. My girlfriend was stunned. She did not understand and she really cut me up. She said, 'I want to go mad with you. Take me with you.' I hesitated, then said, 'I will come back and get you.'

I left the next morning. I think we both knew after we said our goodbyes that both our lives were going to change forever. We continued writing to each other for quite a few months, until my girlfriend wrote saying she was fretting and wanted me to come and bring her back to Yenda. It must have been about October because Yenda was in the grand final of the rugby league competition. It was an important game for Yenda, I wanted to say, 'Hello,' to two of my friends who were in first grade. We had gone to school together. I happened to mention to them I had a girlfriend who I intended bringing to Yenda with me. They were cocky, big-time first-graders, chewing gum, sneering at me, thinking they were really good. They said, 'Introduce us to her, we will F her for you.'

I walked away, disgusted. Saddened and fearful of our future together, I thought Yenda hadn't changed much.

I was working as a railway fireman in Griffith, doing mostly night work, then I would come home and help my grandmother and mother pick carrots or hoe rock melons and pumpkins on our farm.

It was about that time I made up my mind I was always going to be single. It looked like I was going to be left to look after mother and grandmother and was never going to marry. I wrote a letter to my girlfriend saying, 'Forget about me, Aussies and Italians do not get along in Yenda.' Sooner or later, she would call me a *dago* and then three or four years later she would divorce me. I told her to marry an Aussie guy, as I was never going to marry anyone.

She wrote back saying she wouldn't listen to my rubbish

and was coming down with her grandmother. However, she became sick and rang my mother's home in Yenda. She wanted me to come and see her. I wanted to, but mother was adamant in saying I could not go. I think mother wanted me to marry a Calabrese girl who would do as she was told, lie like a log in bed and wouldn't mind if I went out and played up. I didn't get to marry the Aussie girl or a Calabrese girl. Many years later, I married a beautiful South American girl. More about that later. My mother was overprotective.

My girlfriend wrote me another letter saying she was going to do as I told her and go out with other boys. I was melancholy for days. At work, I fired the train through to Narrandera Station. I thought I saw the girl from Lithgow on the platform. She had long, blonde hair and walked exactly the same way. I called out, but when she turned around, it was not her. I then realised she was getting on with her life and I must get on with mine.

It was 1958. I started going wild, drinking, fighting, womanizing. It seemed to be the thing to do. I took to playing rugby league and that saved me for a while. I was in reserve grade for all the season of 1958. I played the five-eighth position.

A lot of friends and people I didn't know would come up to me and say they could not understand why I wasn't playing first grade. But I knew why. Some of the players in the first-grade side were those I had fought against and ran away from at school. They had turned the first-grade coach against me. He too, in my opinion, was racist. Some selectors weren't much better. They were heard to say more than once, 'We had to put the *dago* in; so-and-so never turned up.'

On my twenty-first birthday, I told mother I was going into town to have a beer. While I was there, I was picked on by the first-grade coach, who said, 'I heard you are pretty good with your fists.'

'I suppose I am,' I replied. It was almost on. However, unknown to me, a man named Eno was watching my every move. He stepped in and broke us up and had a word with Mr Jolly. Mother had planned a surprise twenty-first birthday party for me and had asked Eno to go to the hotel and bring me home. I was pleased at the surprise and still proudly have that twenty-first birthday plaque. Most of my friends were there, and it remains one of the highlights of my life.

Back to football

Yenda's brilliant halfback, Mario Guerra, races towards the tryline with Magpies' second rower Bill Hickford in hot pursuit. Guerra could have scored from this run but he failed to pass when he had support and ran

I kept asking the coach to give me a run in first grade. He kept fobbing me off, right until the last game. Yenda had no chance of making the final four. Finally, he said,

'You are in, you are going to get a run in first grade.' I was stoked, I told my mates to come and watch me play first grade. However, just before the game he came to me and said someone else was playing first grade in my place.

Late in 1957, in my own way, I gained my revenge on the ones who did the job on me. One left in a hurry on his motorbike for Queensland. He never came back.

In 1959, there was a new coach. I got picked to play on the wing in first grade for the first trial match. Then I was moved to half back, where I stayed for many years. I won Best and Fairest for the club that year and was told by a selector I would be getting a big trophy. However, I was given a watch and a reserve grader got the trophy.

The following year, 1960, a first-grade coach from Sydney came to Yenda. He was absolutely brilliant; he taught me a lot. His name was Kevin Diett, and he was easily the best footballer I had ever seen or played with. I won the Best and Fairest again that year, sharing the honour with another player. My prize was a valise and the other player received the trophy. It didn't matter: rugby league was an escape for me. It took my mind off things. In that era, Group 20 comprised of towns from Wagga Wagga, Griffith, Batlow, Tumbarumba, Leeton, Yanco, Narrandera, West Wyalong and Temora. Many clubs were able to afford professional coaches and ex-international and first-grade footballers from Sydney.

I was over the moon at playing against great players such as Don Furner, Greg Hawick, Ron Crowe, Brian Hambly, Alan Staunton, Bill Sorenson, Fred Griffiths, Ross Kite, George Smith, George Menzies and many others.

In the sixties, the newspapers would print things like, "On his day, Guerra is the best player in the country," and "Mario Guerra can score a try whenever he feels like it, mercurial, brilliant, Will-o-the-Wisp."

'You'll get picked to play Country against City. You'll play for Australia,' said some of my fans. All heady stuff which had me thinking once again, *if only I can, I will then have enough money to get my dad out of that place.*

But it wasn't all peaches and cream. A Yenda selector gave me heaps in his column, Yenda Yaps & Yelps. "Mario Guerra, hung onto the ball again, jarred the backline, doesn't give the ball out." Maybe I hung on, maybe I didn't. But they never dropped me. I know of two other players who were supposed to hang onto the ball, their names were Allan (Alfie) Langer and Tommy Raudonikis, two of Australia's greatest half backs.

My best year in rugby league was 1960. I was runner-up to John Cann, the Olympian who won the Best and Fairest for Group 20. It was also a good year for romance. I was best man to my cousin Joe Agostino's wedding. I met a beautiful Calabrese girl and we liked each other right away. We were best man and bridesmaid at his wedding. My mother worked overtime, trying to match us up. Her father liked me; her mother didn't. I think she thought her husband might make eyes at my mother, who was a beautiful lady.

The week before, Yenda had played a two-all draw with Tumbarumba in the grand final.

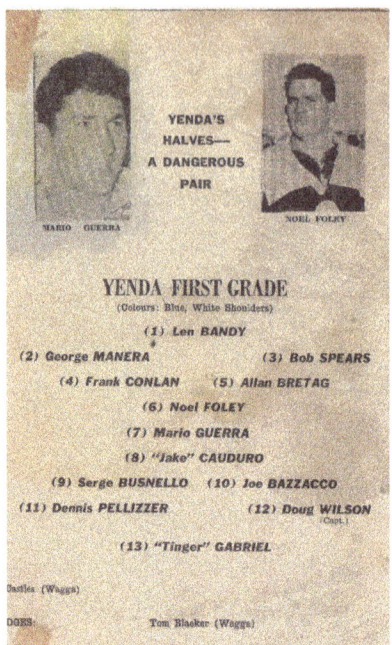

Yenda's first grade of the sixties was a regular line-up of Aussies with Italian names. It was considered normal to have five or six of us in the side. Throughout that era, it was said Yenda's grand final team of 1960 was the best ever.

Yenda's Noel Foley could have played for Australia if he had wanted to. He only had to go and play for a city team. He was absolute brilliance. I rated him alongside Kevin Diett as the greatest player I have ever seen or played with.

The night of my cousin's wedding, I stayed until midnight dancing with my new girlfriend and drinking coffee.

When I arrived home at about 1.00am next morning, I couldn't sleep and the caffeine kept me awake. It got to about 9.00 or 10.00am. I was tired and my feet were sore from dancing. I thought, *Heck, why couldn't we have won the game*

last Sunday? In the first grand final, I was in the clear. The line was in front and I could have scored. But I passed the ball out to the guy outside me, so as to do the right thing and not hang on to the ball. However, in the wet, slippery conditions he dropped the ball and a try went begging. I kept hounding the Tumbarumba coach, Don Furner, taking him high several times but he sucked me into his elbow and I ran into it. I finished up with a badly lacerated mouth. I was lucky to finish with my teeth. It was easily the hardest game of rugby league I had ever played. In the second grand final, we lost 8-4. The game did not reach the great heights of the previous week.

Yenda's grand final team in 1960 played out a two-all draw in pouring rain against Tumbarumba. Extra time was played, with still the same result. The following week, a replay was ordered with Yenda losing 8-4. Right on the bell,

THE AREA NEWS, GRIFFITH, TUESDAY, SEPTEMBER 27, 1960

Yenda and Tumba Meet Again Next Sunday

Grand Final was Amazing Match

By BARRY MOORE

Sunday's 2-all draw between Yenda and Tumbarumba at Narrandera was probably the most amazing Group 20 Rugby League grand final ever played.

Group officials ordered 20 minutes' extra time in an effort to reach a decision. But this failed to break the deadlock and the match will be replayed at Narrandera next Sunday.

Rain reduced the crowd, which paid £582 at the gate. But the Group will collect £400 rain insurance.

This was the second time Yenda has appeared in a grand final and extra time has been ordered.

In 1957, against the Wagga Magpies, the scores were 12 all, and Magpies won the match during the extra time.

Under the conditions on Sunday the match was probably the best exhibition of football seen in Group 20.

The Narrandera ground, which was nothing more than a sheet of water, was subjected to a constant downpour throughout the afternoon and a bitterly cold wind blew across the ground all day.

Even though both teams came out in fresh jerseys after lemons, it wasn't long before it was nearly impossible to distinguish a green jersey from a blue one.

Because of these adverse conditions, and the manner in which both sides played the game, I rate the match as the best I have seen in this area.

Goals were Kicked Early

The scores for both sides were opened very early in the game. Foley landed a goal for Yenda, and minutes later Barry Goldspink raised the flags for Tumba.

Foley and Furner had shots during the match, but the ball was far too heavy to make any kicks look dangerous.

With the scores evened so early in the match, both sides then settled down to score a try, both realising, of course, that it would practically sew the game up if they could cross for the three-pointer.

With this in mind, both sets of players gave all they had to the game, and play seesawed from one end of the ground to the other in great passing bursts and magnificent rucking by the forwards.

Yenda seemed to settle down a little earlier than their opponents, and Foley, Guerra, Breteg and Dahlenburg all played with great combination.

Dahlenburg brought the Blues to their toes several times with some grand runs to see him grounded just short.

It was then Tumba's turn. With the brilliant Furner instigating most movements and receiving great support from Ken Goldspink and Barry Kellham, the Greens started an onslaught on the Yenda line.

The same pattern was apparent during the second half, when once again both sides hammered at the opposition's line in an endeavour to go across.

First it seemed that the Blues must go over, and within minutes it seemed that Tumbarumba must cross.

While all this attacking was going on, the defence of both teams was magnificent.

When players finally did look as if they had found the breakthrough, and started to move through it, a wall of defensive jerseys came across to cut off the movements.

Both sides played the game in such torrid fashion that they were completely exhausted by the time the final whistle had gone.

At one stage players were just falling to the ground when they could see no chance of a breakthrough.

Furner in particular, about ten minutes before full time, received the ball, looked about, and then flopped to the ground.

The spirit in which it was played left no doubt that these two sides were the two deserving to play off in the grand final. Though the game was tough and torrid, not one caution had to be handed out.

The match next week should again be a blinder, with little difference in the scores once again, and anyone's match.

For Tumba, Don Furner was again magnificent.

He received great support in the forwards from Ken Goldspink, who was tireless all day, and Doug Russell, who made some great runs.

In the backs, Kellham, Billy Goldspink played magnificently.

For the Blues, Busnello was again the star with some great running from the rucks. He seemed to be on the ball all day, and was always looking for opportunities.

Longmore, in the tight stuff, was a tower of strength and Jake Cauduro tackled tigerishly all day.

In the backs, Guerra, though receiving a bad lip injury, played extremely well, and once again proved very elusive.

Alan Breteg and Foley in the centres played particularly well, with Foley looking dangerous every time he received the ball.

Dahlenburg on the wing was faultless, and Len Bandy at full back played a magnificent game, with not one fault all day.

He overshadowed his opposition, Barry Goldspink.

The fact that Tumba had more of the ball than Yenda may have had some bearing on the match.

But I still think that these two teams are really well matched, and an epic struggle should eventuate next Sunday.

AROUND THE LEAGUES CLUB

By CLUBMAN

There were some very happy members at the Leagues Club on Sunday night and a lot of tries were scored.

They were the Reserve

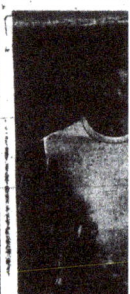

WHO WON?

Week-end competition football matches resulted:
RUGBY LEAGUE GROUP 20. Grand Finals: Firsts, Yenda 2 drew with Tumbarumba 2; Reserves, Griffith 9 d Wagga Magpies 0; Juniors, Griffith 21 d Leeton 0.

SOCCER
Semi-finals: Yoogali Club 3 d Henwood Park 2; Arsenal d R.A.A.F. on forfeit.

Reserves, Juniors

Yenda appeared to score with the corner post knocked out. The try was disallowed by referee Jack Jewell.

Mario Guerra and Jake

With my football friend, Jake Cauduro, we had decided that win, lose or draw against Tumbarumba in the epic grand ginal, we would take a holiday and go to Surfers Paradise.

Things weren't going too well with my new girlfriend. She came from a very strict Calabrese family. She was 16; I was 22. Her parents told me she was too young and I had to wait. We would send letters or give each other a look, or a quick squeeze of the hand. Sometimes she would call me. I dared not phone her; that's how it was. She also said if she got caught phoning or writing to me, her parents would break her legs. Crazy stuff, after the beautiful romance I had in Lithgow. Why did I do it? To please my mother, that's why. Also, she was a good-looking girl, and we liked each other.

Thinking back, I wasn't really one of them, I was too Aussie. I fought in the ring, played football, and my family had a history of mental illness — which was a lot of nonsense. At the most, my father, my uncles and my grandfather were depressed. What they needed was counselling, kindness and understanding. How different it is today. It is said that 50 per cent or more of us are schizophrenic, but lead normal lives thanks to a better understanding of medicine within the community.

I bided my time, playing football and sparring with my mates. I had a fight in the ring at Narrandera in November 1959. From that bout, Ted Scobie challenged me. He had been around, fighting six, eight and ten rounders at Sydney Stadium.

Neither of us knew that the bout was going to become a promoter's dream. The stadium was packed. It was refereed by a former world champion called Jimmy Carruthers. It was over six rounds and was the main event. It was a good fight; the crowd enjoyed it. I was too good for Teddy Scobie.

1960: Ted Scobie, referee Jimmy Carruthers and myself, taken at Yoogali Club at a function after the fight.

Jimmy Carruthers announces Mario Guerra (left) the victor over Ted Scobie, after one of the finest contests ever seen in Griffith.

Things were getting grim with my girlfriend. She became sick and went into hospital. Not being able to see her, I snuck in the back way out of visiting hours. However, the lady in the next bed was also a Calabrese and she told her mother, and that was that. Her mother ordered me never to see her again. We tried for another two years. Her mother couldn't understand her fondness for me when we never saw one another. They even sent one of her cousins to see me, who asked me questions about how it was possible. However, after three years it got too much and it was called off.

I wasn't too upset. I had been taking other girls out to pass the time. One girl in particular liked me a lot. I would take her to the football games and we had a good time. I liked her, but not enough. It was 1962 when I called it off. It frightened me. I thought she was going to do something silly. She was a very nice girl who later married.

I was coaching the Yenda juniors that year. Her brother, who was a star player for the juniors, came up and punched me in the face in front of the Yenda Cafe. I deserved it. However, I punched him back.

'Don't punch me again,' he said. Thankfully, we ended up friends.

In 1963, I became coach of the Yenda Blue Juniors. We got into the grand finals in 1963 and 1964, but was beaten 15-7 and 2-nil. I kept my first-grade position at half back, but was plagued with injuries to my ankles.

Yenda Blue Juniors before their Grand Final against Wagga Kangaroos

I was getting sick of football and going nowhere in life. It seemed I would forever be making wooden boxes or working on that five-acre block. My mother found me down the end of the farm, sitting down in the pumpkin patch, brooding. I told her there were too many memories. They wouldn't go away and I didn't even like Yenda much. Mother said, 'Let's move to Griffith,' so we did. I was happy. We moved into a nice three-bedroom home, with a septic toilet.

We moved to Griffith on Christmas Eve, 1964. I said to mother and grandmother I would see them in Griffith, as I wanted to say goodbye to some of my friends. I said too many goodbyes and too many beers followed at the Yenda Hotel. I was in the lounge when a fellow named Mr McRae clocked me one. It appears he got upset when I put my arm around his wife. He was a big, beefy man and could fight a bit. After a while (about two minutes), I got in a left hook and Peter was out, right out. Immediately after, a fellow called Elliot challenged me. We got into it and he was going all right until a right cross put him down. He got up, but just to make sure, I crashed his head into a brick wall. He too went out, right out. It was Christmas Eve; there were people who came to watch from the main bar; there seemed to be people everywhere.

I was challenged a third time, by a hard man whose nickname was Knuckles. He was big; he was tall. He had booze in him, just like me, and he wouldn't take no for an answer.

He said, 'What's the matter with you?'

I replied, 'Right-o, you big clunk, I'll knock you out too.'

We got into it. I was surprised to find he was easier to handle than the other two, I was having a picnic with him, that was until the long arm of the law grabbed me by the throat from behind, and told me to go home or he would lock me up. I intended to do exactly that; I walked outside to go home, but then I went back looking for my shoes. I found them in the lounge, but I forgot about what the big sergeant had said and went into the main bar to celebrate my victories. Big Knuckles spotted me, let out an angry roar, and grabbed me. He was crankier than a bag full of scalded cats. The hotel was packed, as it was Christmas Eve. With big men, I needed room to move, and I didn't have that advantage. That part of the Yenda Hotel was barely six feet wide and about 20 feet long. I just stayed in close and hung on. He was throwing punches everywhere, but couldn't land one.

He tried to throw me off, but I hung on. He was getting

tired, so was I. The people were so close to us that it was impossible to get in a good one. We stopped, and agreed we would meet at 8.00am the following morning in front of my place. Mother and grandmother would be in Griffith by then and wouldn't know anything about it.

I went outside to go to our house in Yenda, when I was picked on once again. Another big fellow; his name was Johnny and he was slow getting started. He took his tie off very slowly, then his watch even slower. I told him to hurry up or it would be New Year's Day before we started; then it happened; the big sergeant grabbed me saying, 'I thought I told you to go home.' I finished up as a guest of Her Majesty for the night. It was hilarious. As the sergeant opened the door to put me in the cell, a gentleman named Big Tiny walked out, saying 'Thanks, Sarge.'

The sergeant told me to stay there whilst he went looking for the absconder. Where did he think I was going? I was locked up! About an hour later, the sergeant came back with Big Tiny. We kept the sergeant awake for a long time, 'Come on, Sergeant, let us out, we have to go to midnight mass.'

But the sergeant would reply, 'Shut up and go to sleep.'

The next morning at eight he let us out and I rushed to my mother's house to prepare for Knuckles, who had not turned up yet. I phoned my mate to come and give me a rub down. I had a shower and was ready. Shortly after that, Big Knuckles turned up. I came out of the house fast, saying to him, 'You ready?'

He looked surprised, then said, 'Look, my wife will

divorce me if I fight you on Christmas Day. Why not let the urgers just wonder who would've been the best of us?'

I said, 'Okay,' and that was that.

In 1965, after my bout with five irate gentlemen and spending the night in the lock-up, I thought at last I was going to wake up to myself, but no. A cousin of mine said, 'Let's let all the tyres in Yenda down before they come out of the hotel.'

Did we do that silly deed? I am not sure. Maybe we did, maybe he did. But a very angry Big Dick and his brother came to the farm the next day, demanding I own up to the evil deed. *Why always me?* I thought. *Why don't they go after my big cousin?* At the most, I am five-foot, four inches, a legacy of my mother, who was four-foot, ten inches. Of course, I denied it as I was having memory lapses, but Big Dick was persistent. He would ring me in the middle of the night. He would question me every time he saw me. He was driving me crazy. Big Dick and his brother John got me in the Yenda Hotel, late in the evening, and started inquisitioning me again. Dick said if I told him who did it, he would walk away and forget about it.

I replied, 'Right-o, I done it,' and that was that. Big Dick then proceeded to give me a clobbering. He went all right for a while; he kept rocking me with big kicks to my stomach and chin. Every time I would lead with my left to his stomach, which he had plenty of, he would get me with kicks to my face. I switched my attack to his head and things started changing. However, he crashed a *Coca Cola* wooden box over my head and things went his way again.

It must have been a good fight because the local constabulary watched it from outside the hotel. Big Dick was tiring and I was getting my second wind, when he said he'd had enough and poured a bottle of drink over his head. I gave him another one for good measure, then challenged his brother. He did not want any part of it. Luckily for me, the two enforcers of the law had left. No great harm was done, and the barman said it was the best fight he ever saw. The proprietor told me I was a villain, but she loved me. Big Dick, his brother and I all became friends.

It was 1965. I was thoroughly enjoying our new house in Griffith and so was my mother and grandmother. My mother's work at the hospital was only two kilometres away. I continued to go to Yenda to work at a peach orchard I leased. Whilst I disliked farming, I made good money from those peaches that year. I gave football up and played several games of soccer for Hanwood. I also had a fight in a boxing tent at the Griffith Show.

My mother was pleading with me to find a girlfriend and get married. My mother was desperate. Unknown to me at the time, mother had asked a kind Calabrese man if he would find a girl for me. This wonderful man and his wife had sons and daughters of their own. These people were different; they seemed educated and weren't jealous or suspicious. Anyway, he brought women at different times to my home for me to look at. I politely said, 'No,' saying to mother I would find my own true love when the time was right.

I suppose 1965 would have been the best year to do something about dad. My mother had a job at the hospital,

I had the farm in Yenda and grandmother could help look after dad. However, then my beautiful grandmother passed away at the age of 83. My mother was adamant I was to find a wife; she wanted to be a grandmother, and wanted me to forget about dad as he would only be a burden. All we could do was go and see him when we could. About this time, my mother found a bed for dad at a nursing home.

By the time mother had negotiated to get my dad out, the bed had been given to someone else. My dear mother, suffered heartbreak after heartbreak, with a son seemingly disinterested in getting himself married, and also missing out on a bed for dad. Then, in 1970, mother gave me the news that she might lose her job at the hospital. Mother was most distressed; she loved her job. It was a great part of her life. It appeared her niece and mother had gone to the hospital and talked to the matron, telling her not to give my mother work because her son had a farm and was a rich man. Thankfully, common sense prevailed.

I spoke with the matron, explaining it was not like that at all, I certainly wasn't a rich man, and had never owned a farm. 'More likely,' said matron, 'there could have been a touch of envy from the niece and mother,' who never had to work, to my knowledge. I went to my cousin (whom I suspected was involved in the incident) and told her it was not a nice thing to do. My cousin went all quiet, and things were never the same with her and my family again.

From 1965 until 1968, things didn't go well on the farm. I got a job working table service at the Yoogali Club, working two nights a week. I also worked as a doorman at the Yoogali

Club on weekends and the RSL Hall on Friday nights. I became engaged to a sultry Sicilian lass in 1967. Once again, my life and my mother's were to be turned upside down. Right from the start, we would phone each other, and on this particular night, my new girl rang my home and we talked words of passion to each other. The kind Calabrese and his wife came to see my mother and just before they left, they gave me a sad look. I later asked mother what it was all about. Mother looked sad and replied, 'I think they were going to give you a chance to go with their daughter.'

What could I do? What did I do? The wrong move, of course. I decided to stay with the sultry Sicilian.

How embarrassing. Every Sunday we would go to the Hanwood Catholic Club escorted by the mother, the brother, the father, the sister, and my mother, who didn't want to come along. Who paid? Me, who else? I was the laughing stock of my mates.

Shortly after we became engaged, our photo appeared in the local paper. On the other side of the page on the sports column there was an article saying, "Mario Guerra cautioned." It was the result of me being sent off in a football match. My mates gave me a ribbing.

'No more playing up, Mario, you're engaged, you have just been warned!'

The invitations went out for the wedding, but something was wrong. My mother was awfully quiet. I wanted my fiancée to live in our house with my mother. She said, 'Yes.' However, mother was nervous. We were marrying each other for the wrong reasons. But that wasn't it. I finally got it out of mother. She had been diagnosed with breast cancer. I saw my mother's doctor; his name was Dr Welsh. I asked how bad it was. He replied, 'If we don't operate right away, you will lose your mother.'

I immediately did the only thing possible. I went to my fiancée and told her we would have to cancel the wedding for the time being because of my mother's cancer. My fiery girlfriend exploded. Either I marry her as planned, or it was over. I was polite, but firm. She took her ring off, threw it in the garden, and told me to go marry my mother. This wasn't the first time I had been told that. I later found the ring, which had cost $135, and sold it back to the same jeweller for $40. My ex-fiancée sent back the presents I had given her over the 12 months we had been together. I, in turn, sent back the presents she had given me. This included a nice jumper that had shrunk to half its natural size. More about that later.

About two days after our wedding was called off, Dr Welsh operated on my mother. What a mess my mother was. With mother's breast removed, the doctor also had to take the lymph gland out. The front of my mother's body, where there once was a breast, to near my mother's belly button, was a huge cut, stitched up.

I was forever thankful to that great doctor. He saved my mother's life. Between my mother's life-threatening cancer and the end of my engagement, I found it hard to cope. I turned to drink for comfort and let all the peaches drop to the ground on that twenty-acre farm. Mother was taken to Royal Prince Alfred Hospital in Sydney for Cobalt Ray treatment. She was there for three months. I was in debt and sold the house I had recently purchased. I went to see mother many times in Sydney, and after three months she came home. We had to wait five years for my mother to be told she was completely cancer free. I snapped out of my drinking.

In 1970, one of the trucks I purchased was a fifteen-tonne, table-top *Acco Diesel*. We were delivering 15 tonnes of wine to Sydney via the Blue Mountains. I chose the mountains because the railway coordination tax was a law at the time, meaning any freight the railways lost had to be compensated. It was hopeless to compete. I later was to have a hand in getting rid of the unfair tax.

Anyway, driving down Kurrajong in the Blue Mountains, I said to my co-driver, 'These brakes feel spongy,' and then that was it: no brakes. The truck gathered momentum. From the top of Kurrajong down those twisting, turning, perilous curves, being pushed even faster by 15 tonnes of wine. The co-driver kept telling me to jump. I told him to jump. I even forgot to use the hand brake on the side of the seat, or I was too scared to use it. The truck just seemed to be going faster and faster. I kept blowing the horn for cars and trucks to get out of the way, and they did. Somewhere close to Richmond, I pulled on the hand brake ever so slowly. I remember there were cars following to see where we were going to crash. If anyone reading this has gone down Kurrajong mountain, they probably disbelieve my story.

When we eventually stopped, all eight wheels at the back of the truck were red hot. It looked like the top of a volcano had exploded.

My co-driver took one look at the wheels and said, 'That's it, I'm going to church every Sunday from now on.'

I don't know if he did, but I know I did ... for a time. Divine providence had looked after us, of that I am sure.

That was not the first time I escaped death by inches. At the Lithgow Depot we would book off, and walk down Esk Bank to Main Street. There were railway lines crisscrossing everywhere. It was about three kilometres from the depot to Main Street. Most of the work was night work. I was walking about 3.00am, when about halfway to my destination I heard a silent clack. I jumped off the railway track, the carriages missing me by inches. Several railway guards and shunters lost their lives that way at the Lithgow Railway Depot from 1956 to 1957.

Back to Yenda

It was 1970. I purchased a little green truck to deliver parcels around Yenda. By now, I had left the farm. I was happy delivering parcels and beer kegs to the Yenda Hotel and Club. At the time, that's all I wanted to do. Then, a multi-national company out of Wagga came to town and took the beer kegs and cartons away from me. It was my taste of cut-throat business and forced me to look at Griffith as an avenue to making a living. The business grew gradually. I purchased two more small trucks to cope with the freight. I was also offered the Comet Overnight Agency, a subsidiary of a multi-national company, TNT. My first cheque for the week was $13.60. However, the weekly cheques later looked good compared to having to pay rail freight right away. After delivering the parcels, there was a wait of 30 days till payment. The transport business grew fast, too fast. I purchased several bigger trucks. I was to eventually purchase a new M.A.N. diesel semi-trailer on time payments.

A taste of what was ahead happened at Jerilderie. My mother accompanied the driver along with her sister, Theresa, to visit a niece in Melbourne. On the trip back, the semi-trailer, fully laden with beer, rolled over on the corner heading into the main street of Jerilderie. There were beer cartons all over the roadway. The town people of Jerilderie had a picnic; there weren't many cartons of beer left for the insurance company. Thankfully, my mother and aunt had taken a bus back to Griffith from Melbourne.

The business had grown too fast. I was losing control. I had purchased several semi-trailers on time payments. I was plagued with breakdowns and semi-trailers tipping over. It wasn't long before all my semi-trailers were either wrecked or repossessed.

I became desperate. The only staff I had left was a secretary and a worker named Lex. They stuck by me. I would take the newest four-tonne pickup truck to Sydney loaded with carrots or onions every day. Five days a week, Lex would look after the Comet runs and the secretary would take the messages. After about three months of this, I was able to get one of the semi-trailers out of the repossession yards. I drove the semi-trailer for about two years. In the meantime, I was able to get my other semi out of the repossession yards as well and afford a driver. He was a good one. His name was Mick Bonfield. I later was able to afford another truck driver, who was a good one too. Slowly, I was paying off my debts, until he rolled the truck. Perhaps I worked them too hard. It was then I decided to get rid of the trucks, and do what I did best: become a freight forwarder and subcontract the work.

A coal miner's daughter

*Mario Guerra and Caterina Guerra
at Hassens Walls, Lithgow, 1956*

It was in Lithgow I met my first love. Patricia was a coal miner's daughter who came from a good family. They liked me! Young love, best love, how sweet it is. How tragic it was to become. Whilst based in Lithgow, I thought I was in paradise. Apart from Yenda, I had never been anywhere. Lithgow for me was so different. If one wanted to make it, Lithgow could be a very romantic place. There were waratahs growing in abundance in the mountains. Quite often, steaming up the mountains, I would pick the waratahs and take them to my girlfriend. Lithgow is nestled in a valley at the bottom of the Blue Mountains. It had everything: sun, snow and frosts, but most of all, nice people.

Watching the trains go by until 4.00am, the black smoke and white smoke against a sky full of stars and a full moon, was (and still is) an unforgettable experience; something I will never forget. My girlfriend's parents' house was on a higher part of the mountain and had a good view of the trains.

Lithgow, beautiful Lithgow, a tough town. A town possessed with great sporting identities, great friendships and great hotels — I counted 11 in my era. I was a *bodgie* with peg pants and a black jacket. We all dressed the same, parted our hair with Brylcream and danced the rock-and-roll every Saturday night, then danced the Maxina waltz and, of course, the progressive barn dance as well. There was a big building called the Wreck. It was always packed and there were always two bands playing nonstop.

It was a time when, upon arriving, they would take your hat, your scarf and your coat, and put them away until you were ready to leave. How different to Yenda, where there was one hotel, thugs, mugs and some ignorant Italians who would tease my mother, my grandmother and me. Yenda was where, in my young mind, it seemed most Italians had fruit farms and were well off, and most Australians had rice farms and were well off.

Lithgow was a miners' town. Almost everybody seemed to be working in the mines or on the railway. In that era, it was the biggest depot within the state of NSW. They had three, and sometimes four, locomotives pulling those huge loads over the Blue Mountains. It was an awesome sight, those steam trains pulling thousands of tons over the Blue Mountains.

Sometime in 1985, at my work place, I received a phone call. The shock of it all made me almost fall off my chair. It was a call from my first great love, after 28 years. The lass from Lithgow wanted to know how I was. Still in disbelief, I said, 'Lithgow?' and she said, 'Yes.'

I then said, 'Whacky Ferguson?'

She said, 'Yes.'

Whacky was a friend of ours, who was a character in his own right.

It did not take long for us to agree that we had to see each other. Leading up to our reunion, we spent many pleasant times talking on the phone throughout the day and night, reliving our rock-and-roll days and the Lithgow Wreck. We talked about the Lithgow motorbike riders, who followed my girlfriend and me over a ravine. We were playing "Follow the leader". Unfortunately, some of the bike riders got hurt and had to be taken to hospital. I do recall most of us being questioned by the Lithgow police at the station. It was news and made the Lithgow papers.

We talked about my two winning bouts with Cyril Bailey,

a good lightweight of that era. He once fought Griffith's Laurie Murray in a ten-round, semi-main event at Sydney Stadium. Bailey defeated Murray in the ten-round fight of the year.

We talked about the time I was hit by a 1955 Holden driven by a lady travelling from Orange. It happened in a street in Lithgow and the bike was a complete mess and so was I. I was taken to the hospital by ambulance and I spent several days there. I still carry the reminders of the accident today, with a lump on my left elbow and another one on my right back ankle. I did not care who was in the right or who was in the wrong, so long as my mother was not told about it. I remember a lot of skin was missing from my face. I was concerned that I would not be allowed to go on a two-week army bivouac due about six weeks after the accident.

I received the call-up and I spent two glorious weeks at a place called Huskisson, a resort not far away from Bateman's Bay, where once again we played war games with fighter planes firing fake bullets from the air. Our leader was a man we liked to call "Pearshape". He acted his part, barking out orders, firing back at the airplanes with his pistol, and telling us to take cover. We were to spend every weekend with the Citizen Military Forces for two years before our training was completely finished. The thought has crossed my mind: I am now trained to defend some of the racist bastards back in Yenda.

Reliving the euphoria of our wonderful past got too much. We knew once we saw each other we would again try to become teenagers and take up were we had left off

28 years ago. My mother was very happy that at last her son was going to settle down with someone he liked. We tried for almost 10 months to make it work. We purchased a Weimaraner pup and watched him grow up, but it wasn't the same. She had a little girl whose father would phone quite often, so my yearning to have children of my own was always on my mind. We had both taken some heavy blows along life's pathways. We agreed to part on friendly terms and have not seen each other since.

Mario Guerra presents Australian Light Welterweight Title Defence souvenir

Boxing

It was Tuesday 2 November 1979, when the biggest riot ever took place in Griffith's showground. The place was packed when over 1000 boxing fans turned up for what promised to be a splendid night of entertainment. The preliminaries were over and the 10 rounds of boxing by Melbourne's Mick the "Italian Stallion" Gatto and Albury's Reno Zurik had been a crowd pleaser.

The two highly rated heavyweights had turned on the fireworks to whet the appetite of the boxing fans, preparing them for the championship main event about to unfold. In a night of drama, Jeff "Flash" Malcolm retained his Australian Light Welterweight title in sensational circumstances. "Charkey" Ramon, the referee, a former Commonwealth and Australian Light Middleweight Champion awarded the fight to Malcolm on a foul after Melbourne's Frankie Ropis struck Malcolm with a low blow. Malcolm was ruled unfit to continue by the medical doctor and the referee disqualified Ropis. Pandemonium broke loose, with Ropis and his manager approaching Malcolm's corner, abusing him. Ropis was seen to spit in Malcolm's face and, within seconds, fans mobbed the ring. Police and officials climbed into the ring trying to restore order. The uproar inside the ring had been preceded by several scuffles by fans in the crowd. Even Jeff Malcolm, becoming distracted, took time out for several seconds and watched his two girlfriends scuffling in the crowd. The police, judges and officials tried to break up the brawls between the painters and dockers loyal to Ropis and indigenous Coree fans faithful to Jeff Malcolm. They had their hands full. The "rounds girl" disappeared, throwing the placards all over the ring, with one striking Ropis' manager.

My mother attending ringside was quickly taken away. Frank Ropis' manager got the worst of it when he crash-tackled Jeff Malcolm, who was trying to get to Frank Ropis after he had been spat on. One judge trying to stop the melee lost his tooth. The ring announcer kept dodging punches whilst at the same time announcing when the next fight night was to be held. A police sergeant was sent flying through the ring whilst trying to control the mob sympathetic to Malcolm and Ropis. I could only watch, as the promotion seemingly went up in smoke.

Several days earlier, 300 tickets had disappeared from the transport office in suspicious circumstances. In another incident, Frank Ropis' manager was taken to hospital, whereupon his fighter was supposed to have been involved in the incident. This was later denied by the Ropis camp. In yet another incident at the venue (Woodside Hall), an attempt was made to set the place on fire. Subsequently, the police declared that no alcohol would be allowed at future boxing promotions. The promotion should have been a financial success but the 300 missing tickets was the difference.

Perhaps the most successful tournament staged happened at the Griffith Dog Ground. In November 1978, a crowd of 3500 fans turned up to an open-air contest between Griffith's Jeff Malcolm and Baby Cassius Austin. Both were rated highly in world rankings. There were 18 preliminaries on the night with the bouts not finishing until 1.30am the following morning.

Many celebrities attended the occasion. Among them were Rocco "Rocky" and Lucky Gattellari, the referee Gus Mercurio and former world champion Lionel Rose. The eventual winner, Jeff Malcolm, later went on to win the World Boxing Federation (WBF) Light Welterweight title.

Another successful boxing tournament was the one held at Yenda in 1970. A leading boxing trainer from Griffith Police Boys Club, Lyall Jones, ably assisted me. We decided to have a Griffith vs. Yenda boxing night; all funds were to go to Yenda Rugby League Football Club. It was a tremendous night with 25 bouts on the program. The papers said it was the biggest and best show ever staged in Yenda, with $721.71 being donated to Yenda rugby league. In that era, it would have been a sizeable amount of money. The night had everything: great fights in the ring and also in the crowd. One Griffith fighter, busy ducking punches, split his boxing trunks showing his crown jewels to all, much to the laughter of the lassies watching at ringside. In another incident, a referee disqualified two fighters for illegal tactics, then he told them to keep fighting anyway.

Two capable former "glove men" controlled the night's festivities in the ring: Neville Dawson and "Sammy Lang" (real name Salvatore Agresta) who in the professional arena fought a draw with Johnny Famechon. Johnny Famechon later became a world champion. The feast of fighting continued into the early hours of the next morning. The Riverina Lightweight title fight was the main event between Leeton's Tony Peacock and Yenda's Gary "Tiny" Hills. Peacock defeated Hills on points after a close contest; but Hills won the title on the scales when Peacock weighed in overweight.

With my first boxing promotion starting in 1959 when the Catholic school fought the Yenda public school, several bouts were fought by adults. The main event was to be between the Bohemian artist Harold Thornton "Harold the Great" vs. the mystery Dutchman Van Dyke. Harold was extremely mischievous. He was in Griffith and Yenda in 1950s, and in the 1960s he was billed as a wrestler.

In the second round, things warmed up, with Harold the Great taking his clothes off and Van Dyke, his dog, nipping parts of his body. The crowd was in an uproar. Then Harold the Great did the unusual act of baring his backside outside the ring ropes for all the crowd to see. It got too much and Harold the Great was disqualified for using dirty tactics, and Van Dyke, his dog, crowned winner. The crowd was ecstatic, extremely satisfied; even I did not know his opponent was a dog.

Harold Thornton was an extremely talented painter with the brush. He was as famous for his paintings in parts of Europe as he was in Australia. He lived in Holland for about a year, where he made the front page in a full gloss photo of himself in a Dutch magazine. His giant paintings can be seen in a Yenda Winery and until recently at the Yenda Hotel.

I started a boxing gym in Yenda at the old Yenda Diggers Club. It proved popular and kept the young people off the streets. It also kept me out of hotels and gave me an interest. I trained myself and the lads on and off for many years, taking them to several tournaments, but it was not until Jeff Malcolm came to town in 1978 that I became serious about promoting boxing. At that time, Malcolm was trained and managed by Steve Knox, who was to lead him to a Commonwealth and Australian title victory in Melbourne. With a high-profile fighter now in the camp, it gave me the encouragement to open up my own gymnasium in Griffith's Banna Avenue.

The gym was successful, developing one NSW Amateur Middleweight champion, Bill Smith. He went on to fight Phil McElwaine, with the winner picked to go to the 1988 Seoul Olympics. The fight was eventually won by McElwaine on points. Also, four fighters went on to win professional Riverina titles. They and others fought main events in Sydney and Melbourne, as well as appearing at other venues throughout NSW. I had two fighters cross swords with a World Amateur Champion in Dubbo; another fought for the NSW Professional Middleweight title in Young, whilst another, Mario Rizzeri, was rated nationally as the number two Professional Super Bantamweight contender, and left for Sydney to further his career.

It was Jeff Malcolm who breathed life into a boxing-starved Griffith. If it were not for him, I doubt if I would have bothered to take on the daunting task of training, managing and promoting fighters.

One of the highlights of my foray into boxing was managing to snare a fight for Jeff Malcolm against world rated number four lightweight contender, Elselso Esmero. The bout took place in Port Moresby, New Guinea. It was a 10-round main support bout to a World Featherweight title fight. Malcolm was too good for Esmero that night and won easily on points.

It was back to Griffith, where the wise-cracking, colourful Jeff Malcolm stayed at my mother's house for several weeks. He was a non-drinker and non-smoker, and was always polite to my mother. He came along to several church meetings. This was another side to Jeff Malcolm that most people did not know.

Barry Michael, another future world champion, visited mother's house for a coffee after the Ropis vs. Malcolm bout. Another time, the great Tony Mundine dropped in for a coffee. He was one of Australia's finest middleweight boxers; this was about as good as it got for me in boxing.

I was to continue managing, promoting and developing fighters until 1982, when my affair with boxing came to an abrupt end. It was either continue with boxing and my business would disintegrate, or leave boxing altogether and save the transport system. I had no choice. My bread and butter, the business, put food on the table and that was the only way to go. Sadly, my fighter Bill Smith was to be matched with Bernie Hall's Australian Champion, Ken Salisbury, for the Commonwealth Light Middleweight title, but everything had to be cancelled.

A highlight for me was being taken to King Island, about 100 kilometres off the coast of Tasmania, by a wrestling promoter named Larry Memerey. He put on a wrestling and boxing show on the island. We flew across in a seaplane from Melbourne with all expenses paid by Larry. It was to be my first trip overseas. Shortly after the Ropis fracas, I went to New Guinea, courtesy of Jeff Malcolm. I was able to secure the fight on a world title promotion, and these were the only times I would venture overseas.

Boxing can be a tough, cruel sport, but it was my drug. I was hooked. For example, I had arranged a fight for Jeff Malcolm against his leading contender, Melbourne's Jimmy Brown. It was to be a non-title contest. For whatever reason, Jeff thought this was going to be an easy fight, so much so that I had to take him off a "pepper" on the early morning of the fight. Pepper in fight talk means a hot chick.

On the morning of the fight, travelling to Melbourne the colourful Malcolm was quoted as saying, 'That's not Jimmy Brown, that's Jimmy Black and Blue; that's what his new name will be after I've finished with him!'

However, it was anything but that. It was an exciting fight with Malcolm winning on points. Jeff Malcolm decided to fight the fighter instead of using his natural boxing ability.

Although Jeff won rather easily, it was Jeff who finished looking the worse for wear and tear.

Other fight jargon I was to learn was, for example, 'See that chap, Mario, he's a "dudder". See that other fellow, he's a "dip", but I will never "dip" or "dud" you, Mario.' I think that was Jeff's way of saying he respected me.

It is over now and I don't for a minute regret my involvement with boxing. From the first time I put on a glove in 1956 doing national service until I gave up the boxing in 1982, I have enjoyed the memory. Boxing and national service taught me to become a man. It was boxing that taught me not to be afraid. It was boxing that taught me to stand up to the mugs. When I came back to Yenda from Lithgow, in one sweet instance I put the gloves on with a man I once feared.

One of my great joys in sport was becoming a successful boxing trainer. My endeavours bagged me four Riverina champions, one NSW State Champion Amateur, and an attempt against a great champion, to fight for the right to represent Australia at the Moscow Olympics. My fighter, Bill Smith, lost by one point. It was ever so close.

I have included a full report written by the *Area News* reporter, Mike Donaldson. Billy Smith was easily the best fighter I ever developed. He had the heart of a horse, he trained the house down, he listened to instructions and was forever loyal. Read on.

SMITH PLANS TO GIVE THE CHAMP THE CHOP

It's 6 am at Griffith's Jubilee Park, and Bill Smith has already worked up a sweat as he pounds around the perimeter of the tree lined ovals.

An elderly woman walks an equally elderly Labrador across the grass, and for a moment a fight threatens as paths are crossed with a man exercising three greyhounds.

But Smith, a 23 year old with blonde hair and the hollow, pale features of a person in superb physical conditions, runs on without noticing, for he has other things on his mind. In seven days, he will step into the boxing ring for his most important toughest contest of his short professional career.

The man he will face on Sunday is NSW middleweight champion, Con O'Connor, of Sydney, known as The Cobra because of his lightning fast left jab. O'Connor who has not been afraid of making known his disdain for Smith's boxing ability is, according to Smith's trainer Mario Guerra, the complete professional who neither drinks nor smokes and who "practically lives in the gym."

O'Connor successfully defended his title in March against the tough Greg Crowe, of Berrigan, who shared the honours with Smith in a bruising training bout earlier this year at Griffith.

Smith runs on, with seven kilometres to cover before he can rest, and the sun's rays beginning to creep over the park's eastern pines. He has been waiting a year for his chance at O'Connor.

● ● ●

"This is the biggest fight I have ever had, the most important one.

"I've been training non-stop for about a year now, with really hard training in the last month.

"Whenever you're running, or skipping or whatever, this fight stays always in the back of your mind.

"You train and sometimes you think 'why am I doing this for?' You want to stay in bed lots of times I think of Con O'Connor, and I think may be in a round when I start to get puffed, this run will get me through.

"I always think of how I'm going to feel after the fight if I lose because I haven't trained. When I don't feel like training, I imagine myself in a fight and getting a hiding. Then I feel like training.

"Being unfit is the only thing that frightens me about boxing. It makes it harder then."

Smith is joined on his run around the park by a lone jogger, whom he quickly passes and leaves lagging in the distance. Trainer Guerra, who religiously attends all his early morning sessions, has been watching his fighter like an anxious horse trainer watching trackwork before a big race.

He calls Smith in on the next lap to begin the classic fighter's preparations, wood-chopping. While the boxer wields the heavy axe over a weathered iron hard log on the edge of the park, Guerra counts off the blows.

Smith begins to grimace under the strain but sticks to the task, attacking the log as if settling an old score.

He is in flight ('O'Connor at Young All Services' Club and Guerra took Smith to Young yesterday), he hopes that separating the boxer from his wife, children and the rest of his family in Griffith will make him mean" for it is the lack of the so called killer instinct in his fighter that concerns him most of all.

The wood chopping count nears that target of 150 and at 149 the blonde James in the tough timber Smith, nearing exhaustion, grabs the handle with final anger, and his final blow is the hardest of all. Guerra smiles with satisfaction.

● ● ●

"My last fight about a month ago, against Willis Diehl water was probably my hardest yet. I wasn't left enough, I was ready to chuck it in in the sixth round. I was fit — not as fit as I am now but fit enough to fight. I just wasn't in the mood, not right men-

tally."

"Lyn, my wife, said if I walk out for this fight the same as I did in the last one, she'd never come and watch me again. Lyn and my Mum, they could tell. I just couldn't be bothered.

"I got beaten on points in that one.

"I got seven stitches and he got six. My legs felt really heavy and when he was hitting me I had to think well. I'd better move.

"After the fight, after we'd been bashing each other, we went down in the hospital together, and had a bit of a joke. We got on really well.

"A lot of times it's a queer sport because you belt them and then afterwards you go off together and have a beer or something."

The sun has cleared the trees as Smith goes into his exercise routine, continually urged on by Guerra. He does 20 Rocky-style one arm push ups before launching into a series of sprints. He is dressed in a Yenda Rugby League jumper, and played in the club's first grade team which won this year's Group 20 premiership.

He finishes his sprints, takes several deep breaths and crouches down into his fighting stance, head held low, shoulders hunched, to shadow box several lengths of the field.

The lone jogger continues around the park and makes a joke about being nearly fit enough to be Smith's next opponent in the ring.

Guerra begins to slow down the pace of the workout and offers his charge a few words of praise. Smith, who appeared a couple of times on the point of exhaustion, recovers quickly and the morning session is over.

It's 7.30 a.m. and after an hour and a half of non-stop training, Smith is ready to begin work for the day as a joiner.

● ● ●

"I do get nervous, but mainly just before a fight. I don't think I worry about it all the time.

"It's 7.30 a.m. and after an hour and a half of non-stop training, Smith is ready to begin work for the day as a joiner.

"Nerves don't worry me that much — it's good fun.

"It's safer than football and a lot of other sports. It's not as

rough.

"When you're busting you've only got one bloke to worry about. But in football you've got to worry about 13 other blokes hitting you.

The couple of days before a fight, when I stop training, I don't know what to do with myself because I'm used to training every night.

"I usually go to bed pretty early — I hate T.V. I can't watch that, I can't sit still in one spot like, say, sitting down and playing monopoly or something. It's alright for about five or 10 minutes but then I get edgy.

"I think I've always been like that.

"At work the other day, I noticed when I went to go down under something, I started ducking and weaving automatically, like I was boxing in the ring.

"Getting a bit carried away, I suppose."

● ● ●

It's 6.30 pm and Smith and Guerra have arrived at John's Health Spa and Gym in Banna Avenue for the evening workout.

It's a far cry from the fight gyms depicted in movies, with its plush carpet, bright colour scheme and disco music blaring.

Smith appears from the change rooms wearing a plastic garbage bag (like a t-shirt The regulars at the gym hardly give him a second glance as he begins his routine. They've seen it countless times before.

Guerra and Smith go into the tiled area near the spar pool where Smith begins a monotonous round of skipping.

He dances up and down the floor with surprising grace and occasionally breaks into 15 second skipping "sprints" at Guerra's command.

He stares fixedly at the brick wall ahead and finally is allowed to stop. Guerra rushes up to him with a towel and mops his face. The garbage bag has done its work well, for the boxer is a lather of sweat.

Guerra talks to Smith all the time in the gym, urging him on, occasionally praising and occasionally critical. He never lets him stop for a mo-

ment.

Smith takes on the heavy punching bag, and the grace of the skipping is gone as he

Bill Smith wields the axe in preparation for his State title challenge.

attacks it with heavy blows. He demonstrates his most effective punch, a looping right hand designed to clear O'Connor's left jab and crash into his face. The blow lands on the bag with a heavy thud.

"Why did I take up boxing? To get back at my sisters — with a few of them you've got to learn to look after yourself. I used to get belted up a lot."

Smith moves around the bag trying to set up combinations of punches with the speed and power he will need if he is to beat the champion.

When he starts to flag, Guerra screams O'Connor's name and Smith attacks the bag with renewed vigour. Guerra runs over to the bag and grabs it, putting his shoulder behind it to take the impact of the punches. He comes perilously close to feeling first hand just how well he has developed his punch landing with right punch. He leaves the bag and lets Smith continue alone

At the end of the bag sessions, Smith is visibly distressed.

Guerra sprays him with water from a plastic bottle, coaxing and cajoling him for more effort.

Smith next attacks a small leather ball suspended between floor and ceiling. He beats a steady tattoo on the quickly moving target, nearly every punch landing with perfect timing.

After several rounds of shadow boxing and some sparring with Guerra, he toughens his stomach muscles by lying on his back while the trainer drops a large medicine ball on him from waist high — 100 times Boxing is a team effort.

"When you see the bloke you're fighting is hurt, you've got to keep going until he drops because it's not as hard then.

"You don't have to come out for the next round and get stuck into him again.

"But if you let him go he might end up getting stuck into you.

"When I know I've got a bloke I just keep going, make sure he's finished.

"Through a fight you feel buggered and you want to stop but then when you've won, everything's gone — you don't remember being puffed you just remember I threw this good punch, I threw that good

punch.

"You don't remember the bad parts. You feel like you've got heaps of energy and could go again.

● ● ●

Smith is really on the comeback trail, after giving amateur boxing away about 18 months ago.

After a handful of fights in the amateur ranks he won his way into an Australian title bout, but lost on points.

He has already had 10 professional fights this year. He has improved to such a degree that Les Gibbons, editor of the boxing magazine, 'The Small Glove News, believes the fight on Sunday will be one of the best of the year. He says Smith is up with the finest boxers in N.S.W. and has a great chance against O'Connor.

● ● ●

"Marlo's seen O'Connor fight. He leans on the ropes and covers up all the time.

"He tries to make his opponent wear out by punching themselves out. He's always jabbing his left out — that's what he used mainly, just to keep you off.

"He's not a bad boxer but I don't think he can take a hard punch.

"I'm going to fix him, I think".

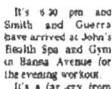

Terry Reagan

In 1982, there was a boxing promotion on. It was normal practice to put boxing placards at hotels and clubs, or other places where people congregated. At one particular hotel, they kept on disappearing and getting ripped up. I knew who it was, as I was expecting a challenge and it came. The first time was at the Griffith Leagues Club. I was picked on and jeered at by Terry Reagan. He was obliged; I offered to fight him right away. I wanted him to have his revenge, but it was not to eventuate because in an earlier incident the manager ordered me off the premises.

Seven weeks later, we met again. This time it was at the Area Hotel. Again, I was picked on by Terry Reagan, and again I offered to fight him. Terry walked away, saying to me, 'I will pick the time and the place.' I noted there were two former Yenda toughs in the bar, as well as other patrons.

The showdown had to come. I knew him to be a tough man, seemingly afraid of nothing. He asked for and gave no quarter on the football ground. A born-and-bred Griffith man, Terry Reagan was a talented rugby league footballer playing first grade in the forwards for the Griffith Black and Whites. I noted he ran strong and hard with his chin up, seemingly causing him to get knocked out several times. One such time was as at a Griffith Black and Whites vs. Waratahs game, this time by a Tony Nardi playing for the Waratahs. I did not think Terry Reagan would last long playing that brand of football. How wrong I was. He went on to play first grade for the Canberra Raiders and for the Sydney City Roosters in the Winfield Cup. He made the front page of a Sydney rugby league magazine. The *Rugby League Week* showed him in an action shot; he was in full Rooster uniform. It happened on a Friday. I was to venture to a nightclub called Regimes at the top end of Griffith's Banna Avenue. It was at a time when I was living by myself.

Although I had a business and a boxing gym to go to after hours, something was missing from my life. I was bored and lonely. I had turned to drink for comfort and in the two previous weeks I had been booked for drink-driving after leaving a club at Hanwood. My venture to Club Regimes is still spoken of today. I walked straight into Terry Reagan and two of his friends, Kerry Hemsley and Tom Mitchell; heavyweights, the three of them. At the time, I believe Kerry Hemsley was a first-grade footballer for Balmain and Tom Mitchell played some football with the Griffith Black and Whites. I understand he went on to become a union advisor with the NSW Building Union. The evening started off well enough with Reagan inviting me over for a drink. As the evening wore on, I noticed they were talking among themselves.

I recall Terry came over to me and said, 'Why did you do it?'

I will now attempt to explain to the reader why the vendetta started in the first place. Some two months earlier my cousin and I were drinking at the Leagues Club.

We were very much under the weather and became involved in a disagreement with several patrons. The barman told us to leave. We went on arguing with him as well. The big barman called the manager, who banned us both from the club premises. It was a bad time for me with the transport business on the verge of falling over. I fell easily into the clutches of the evil demon, drink.

We ventured from the Leagues Club to an Italian restaurant named La Scala at the top end of Griffith's Banna Avenue. Walking down the stairs in front of the door to the restaurant was Terry Reagan and another chap, nicknamed Charger. They were punching and wrestling each other on the ground. There was a crowd in attendance, so much so that it made it difficult to enter the premises with these two scrappers blocking the doorway. Nature was calling me in my inebriated state. I blamed the two pugilists for my discomfort and passed urine on the pair of them. It is not clear what happened next, except the two fighters got up from the ground. I was told that I hit Terry Reagan or somebody. But from then onwards, the legend was born.

'Why did you do it? It was not the thing to do,' said Terry. He, of course, was right. I often wonder what if the situation had been reversed and someone had urinated on me, what would I have done? Perhaps in the heat of the moment I would have retaliated and maybe after I had cooled off, I would have laughed about it, as Terry Reagan's opponent did.

'Why did you do it?' Terry kept asking me at the club at Regimes. The beer and the whisky kept flowing and we kept on talking. I tried explaining to Terry that it was only a joke. Why didn't he look at it that way? But Terry kept brooding and thinking. He was being urged on by his two heavy mates, or so it appeared. The night wore on and finally Terry said, 'We will fight, Mario, I know you for a man and you won't go to the cops.'

I agreed. I recall telling Terry, 'If you want me so bad, we can go out the front now in a fair fight or we can go up the hill in the morning.'

But Terry kept thinking. At that, I thought I had talked Terry around, but as I went to the gents, I was followed inside by the three of them. I wanted to prepare myself for what was about to happen. I thought I was going to be belted inside the toilet. I wasn't. I walked out of the gents and told a mate, 'I am going to cop it tonight. Watch my back.' He didn't.

I went and had a dance and after that I went to go home, thinking, *if it happens it happens*. The lady proprietor went to open the door but she did not quite make it before the heavy door fell on me. Or was it a truck? No, it was Terry Reagan.

With my back to Terry, the roof fell in, or that's how it felt when the punches rained down on the back of my head. I remember going down low, then turning around. I ducked to escape his punches, but he straightened me up with kicks from his knees. My face was starting to swell. I stood up and caught Terry with two good punches.

That was when Tom Mitchell grabbed me and threw me out the door, saying, 'If you want to fight, fight outside.' He was a strong man and threw me hard. I remember rolling on the cement five or six times. I picked myself up, only to be crash-tackled by Terry Reagan into a large Regimes' plate glass window. Everything came crashing around us; there was glass everywhere. We either jumped out into Banna Avenue or fought our way out. Terry came at me again. I remember sidestepping him and trying to get my shoes off at the same time, but he was too quick and crash-tackled me again. As we hit the cement hard, Terry had me on the ground, scratching and biting me. I managed to kick my shoes off and remembered Terry biting me on the thighs, my backside, my face and my head. I remember Terry trying to scratch my eyes out. This was my welcome to new-age street fighting.

We both got up from the ground. I was now in the open when Terry rushed at me again. I sidestepped him but Terry rushed at me again, leading with his chin. I hit him with a beautiful short right. Terry Reagan went down and was knocked right out. There was a great roar from the crowd; the fight was turning my way. It was then I did a strange thing. I bent down and said, 'Come on Terry, you can still beat me.'

At that stage, I was convinced I had the better of Terry Reagan, but almost immediately Terry bounced up. Why did I do it, that's the question I ask myself until this day? Why didn't I rub Terry Reagan's face in the cement or grab him by the ears and belt him to the stormwater drain where he lay? I had about four seconds before Terry got up, but get up he did. I danced around him while he threw his wild punches. By now, we had both slowed down and not many punches were thrown. I recall moving towards Terry, trying to set him up for one more big right.

Terry Reagan was waiting for me.

I am sure at that stage he was as tired as I was. I threw a slow straight left; Terry moved back and made a funny noise. He said, 'Tell the crowd you are sorry.'

I said, 'No,' and gave him a four-letter word. I advanced again, but Terry was too tired to come after me.

It was then that Terry did a strange thing. He turned around and ran, saying, 'I am coming back in three years to get you.' If that was to be the case, I would be the ripe old age of 48. Terry was, at that time, 25 years old and I was 45.

Two theories why Terry Reagan ran away: he may have been worried the police would come or he may have been worried he was going to walk into another big right punch.

What about me? Why didn't I do to Terry Reagan what he had done to me? My theory is I have always believed in a fair go. If your opponent gets knocked down, let him up, then have a beer after it is all over.

Another theory was, perhaps I wanted Terry to beat me. I would have preferred that, rather than having to fight his two goon mates who were forever hovering around during the battle. I enjoyed that fight; it remains a highlight. If it had not been for the attack from the back, I think the fight could have finished much sooner.

The prognosis after the fight from people who watched was that Terry Reagan did not beat me that night, but I am happy for Terry Reagan to gain his revenge.

My mother's social life

In 1982, my mother was on long service leave from her work at the hospital. Uncle Lorenzo, who married my mother's youngest sister, asked mother if she would like to go to Italy for a holiday. My mother said, 'Yes' and spent an enjoyable two months visiting my father's relatives in the Northern part of Italy. She also went to Calabria and visited the land of her birth, at a township called Ionica.

Whilst over there with my uncle and her sister, they visited the Madonna in Lourdes. My mother happily spent the months of May and June in Italy. However, according to my uncle, it was disappointing to see my mother and his wife not being able to get along whilst on holiday.

My mother's 26 years working at the Griffith Base Hospital filled her with pride. She would say often, 'It is my social life, son.' She would get up in Yenda at 5.30am to prepare herself for work in Griffith, which started at 7.00am. Every morning, she would cross a dangerous Yenda bridge, which was a worry during the foggy winter mornings. My mother was to make many friends during her employment and was saddened when at 65½ years it became her time to retire.

When the Italian weddings were on, mother would wash dishes for a kind Italian man, a Mr Don Zaccaria, on weekends. Mother would come home after the weddings tired but happy. She quite often would be given some of the wedding leftovers: pieces of chicken, cakes, etc. We were invited to many weddings in that era, mostly my grandmother's grandchildren and relatives.

Calabrese wedding in the 1960s

The "festas" or "fetes" were something in that era. They were very popular in Yoogali, Yenda and Hanwood. Mother loved them.

When mother bought her first radio, she was over the moon. She seemed to be forever listening to *When a Girl Marries*, the news, and the funeral announcements.

Mother and grandmother were devoutly religious and would join in the processions around the churches and schools.

Only 300 people were invited to Calabrese weddings in the 1960s. My mother and grandmother were extremely popular with both the Southern and Northern Italian community.

Mother, grandmother and I would be invited to Christmas parties. We would go to a different sister every year. She also liked to visit her friends and neighbours.

About 1965, the year my grandmother passed away, things changed and mother only wanted to go to her second youngest sister's Christmas party. Mother also made sure we visited the Guerras in Victoria. There was a definite bond between her and my father's relatives.

When my dear mother retired and was in her seventies, I would ask her if she wanted to go to a movie or to a concert. She would reply, 'Oh, son, I have had my social life, I don't need to go out anymore.' Of course, her social life was what I have mentioned.

I do know my mother loved visiting the Guerras in Victoria. She would say, 'You work too hard, son,' but what

I think she really meant was, 'I would love to visit your relatives in Victoria.'

I was trapped in a terrible business I could not get out of.

Towards the end, my mother was content to just watch television. Mother lived next door to us and most of the time we would watch television at her place with my wife and children. Of course, when my mother became extremely sick, she wouldn't watch anything.

My grandmother, Maria Natalina Agostino

Celebrities

My mother quite often asked me, 'Have any of our relatives become celebrities?' Even at home on her deathbed, weeks before she passed away, she asked me this question.

I would reply, 'Yes mother, we do have one. He is on the Guerra side and is a nephew to Jimmy. He plays first grade football, Australian Rules, for St Kilda in Melbourne.'

I went on to tell her he looked a lot like dad when my father was very young. My mother seemed content. My mother had taken a battering from the cruel jibes of ignorant people. She wanted one of our relatives to make it in the celebrity world, thereby proving we were just as sane as the next person.

Apart from Brent Guerra in Aussie rules, there was a Mick Agostino who made it in rugby league, starring in a premiership winning side for the Griffith Waratahs. There were the three Guerras at Ballarat representing Victoria against Northern Territory in polocrosse. They were beaten by the Waratahs. In the side for the Waratahs was Yenda's Don Stockton. In the losing side were Les, Jimmy and Johnny Guerra that year.

Roslyn Guerra held, until recently, the 100-metre Junior National Sprint championship. She once ran with Raelene Boyle, a future Olympic and Commonwealth champion. Roslyn is the daughter of John and Betty Guerra. It's interesting to note the four Guerra girls and two Guerra brothers all married into Australian-born families, with John Guerra, son of my father's brother, migrating from Italy to marry his Australian sweetheart, Betty.

My mother was pleased to know one of her sister's children had married a politician from Canberra. Another married a dean from Bathurst and became a successful music teacher, whilst another granddaughter married a policeman.

Records

At the moment, there was a regular first grade member playing for the Leeton Greens. He was a member of the 2004 grand finalists being defeated by Yenda in the Group 20 competition. Again in 2006, he was a first-grade member of the Leeton vs. Yenda grand finalists, being narrowly defeated by the all-conquering Yenda Blues.

I think my mother had high expectations of me. She tried very hard to get me to become a priest. Being an altar boy most of my school life, I was keen. However, my mother found she could not afford the high cost of educating me. She then asked if I would consider becoming a monk, as that was affordable. I wasn't interested at that point of time. My mother had suffered so much. She didn't want me to go through the same thing she did. How wise my mother was, with the stigma of insanity, being mocked at, laughed at, being forever poor, she loved me too much; I was fortunate for that.

Mother then wanted me to become a singer, telling me dad had a beautiful voice. I liked singing and still do. However, I was inexperienced and didn't have the right connections. How far did I go in singing? Nowhere!

The nuns would get me to sing in the church choir. I remember the song on my First Communion day, singing it for several years. The school plays were great; I remember singing The Desert Song. I sang almost every day at home.

I liked singing romantic songs, country and western, and Italian songs. I would be asked to sing at football presentation nights at parties. My favourites were Mona Lisa and Lonely Boy. In 2003, I hit the airwaves of Griffith singing One Ton for Guerra. It was simply a business ad and it went over well. Shortly after, my mother became extremely sick.

War and the Depression

With the war raging and with the Depression, how did any of those people survive? The determination to live and not give up, by both the Australian and Italian communities, fills me with awe.

I find myself asking, could our councils do more? Perhaps give those wonderful pioneers citizenship of the year, every year, even some posthumously? I read a book about Beelbangera from 1788-1988 called *Beelbangera: where the brolga roamed*. I found it an extremely interesting book and would thoroughly recommend it to anyone who would like to know more about the history of Griffith.

One of the articles the book mentions is an excerpt written by Bob Fanshaw. He goes on to say, "During the war the troop train with men, guns, trucks, etc., would pass through Beelbangera night and day."

Bob Fanshaw's dad had a hard-mouthed horse, only half broken in, who was a bolter. He called him Phar Lap.

Paul Guerra, who lived opposite Fanshaw's in Davis Street, arranged to borrow the horse to go into town and see the priest to make plans for his forthcoming wedding, which, of course, was to my mother. He turned up in his Sunday best. Bob Fanshaw's dad saddled Phar Lap, legged Paul Guerra on board and away he went. A short time later, Phar Lap was back all covered in sweat. He had taken Paul to town, straight past the church and back home again without stopping. Paul, my father, kept saying, 'He no stop, he no stop.' Paul looked very relieved to get off.

Another excerpt written by Joe Bicego from the same book goes on to say, "There was definite contention between the Australians and the Italians." Take our case for example. We took over a soldier settler's farm and were accused of taking his farm away, which was not true as we had bought it. There was an even number of Italians and Australians and even though there was dissention, we eventually all learned to live together. It was sort of a three-way split. For example, Dad came from Northern Italy and then there were the Southern Italians and then the Australians. The kids used to get together, but the older people would put up barriers telling Northern kids to keep away from Southern Italian kids, and the Australian kids were told to keep away from all Italians. The Irishmen used to cop it all until the Italians came along.

My father's brother had failing health and visited his brother several more times before he died at an early age. I have fond memories of my mother taking her mother and me to Koondrook to stay at my uncle's dairy farm, where we would milk the cows and I would help to pitchfork the hay onto the big horse-drawn trailer. My cousins turned two wheels upside down and made a merry-go-round, much to the enjoyment of my mother and grandmother.

I went to school for two weeks at Cunnawarra and saw my first pickled snake in a bottle. I remember it taking us two-and-a-half days to get to Koondrook from Yenda by train. I remember being stranded at Tocumwal, a border town this side of New South Wales, and lodging with my mother and grandmother at a boarding house where I received my first big breakfast. I seemed to go for the toast and marmalade a lot. The neat serviettes, the nice tablecloths, the fancy teapots and plates and the nice people; I was a young boy and remained starry-eyed at the whole thing. We were then put on another train full of meat carcasses with several other men. Mother never had to pay; I think it's called "riding the rattler". The men told us where to get off, whereupon mother made arrangements for someone to take us to the Guerra dairy farm.

Whilst my stay was most enjoyable, I also remember men on horses with guns watching over Italians in chains. They must have been prisoners-of-war or from concentration camps working on a channel. I remember at night-time the guards allowed the prisoners to congregate at the Guerra household. One man would play a guitar and everyone would join in the singing. I remember the Guerras taking my mother, grandmother and me by horse and gig to see the movies at Barham, over the Victorian Koondrook bridge. They also took us to Swan Hill, once again by horse and gig.

Our cousins, aunts and uncles were extremely kind to us. There were five sisters and two brothers. Even at my young age (I must have been about eight), I had a crush on my female cousins, probably because they were being just what they were supposed to be: girls. The boys would tease me a bit, but we got along fine. As I was growing up, my mother took me to visit them several times. They, in turn, came and visited us quite a few times in Yenda.

My Uncle Peter came to visit us in Yenda. I recall we were picking carrots on the farm and it was raining. We kept picking the carrots, protecting ourselves with sheets of aluminum roofing on our back. I remember another uncle, my mother, grandmother and me doing what I thought was natural, that was, continue working. Uncle Peter helped until it rained. Then he went home to get out of the pouring rain.

In royal company

I will never ever be able to comprehend why much, much more was not done about the plight of my father, my two uncles and my grandfather. The end result was that people would always know and talk about our family, no matter how much it was swept under the carpet. The taint of insanity would not leave us. In our youth, we would have discussions about why we would or would not go mad.

However, we are in royal company if we are to believe a newspaper clipping written in the *Daily Telegraph*, Tuesday, 7 April, 1987. On page nine it says in bold print, "Queen shunned cousin in an asylum London: A cousin of the Queen has spent the last 40 years shunned and shut up in a mental hospital, it was claimed yesterday." The locked-up woman's sister, also mentally handicapped, is buried in an untended pauper's grave.

The cover-up involving Katherine and Nerissa Bowes-Lyon was exposed by Britain's *Sun* newspaper yesterday. The women are first cousins of the Queen, nieces of the Queen Mother, and aunts of top photographer Lord Litchfield. They have been listed as dead since the 1963 edition of *Burke's Peerage*, the Who's-Who of the British monarchy and aristocracy. Yet, Katherine was very much alive. She is a long-term patient in the state-run Royal Mental Hospital in Redhill Surrey, once savaged in a Government report for its lack of sanitation.

Nerissa also spent most of her life there before dying, aged 67. A hospital insider said, 'Neither of the sisters has been visited by their family in living memory. They have certainly not received any royal visitors.'

A staff member said Katherine existed on a State Pension of a few pounds a week and her only possessions were a few hospital clothes and some worthless items in her locker.

Nerissa is buried in Redhill Cemetery. The only clue to the aristocratic occupier of the grave is a tag bearing the name Bowes-Lyon and a reference number attached to a plain white cross. Her death certificate showed she was a victim of pneumonia and severe mental deficiency. Genealogist Hugh Peskett blamed the sisters' mother, Fenella Bowes-Lyon, for the alleged cover-up. The sisters were listed as alive in the 1959 edition of *Burke's Peerage*, yet four years later it recorded Nerissa's supposed death in 1940 and Katherine's in 1961.

'I can only imagine she (their mother) was responsible,' Mr Peskett said.

When Nerissa's eldest sister, Princess Anne of Denmark, died in 1980, the Queen, the Queen Mother and many of the other royals attended a memorial service.

The usual burial place for Bowes-Lyons is at the 14th Century Glamis Castle in Scotland. Neither Nerissa nor Katherine were made beneficiaries of a trust fund by their parents.

Cary Grant, the Hollywood actor of the 1940s, 50s and 60s, did quite the reverse: he got his mother out of a mental asylum. His mother went on to live a normal life. He did not find out until 20 years after his ninth birthday, according to his autobiography.

My first employment

Somewhere in mid-1951 at the age of 14, I left school to go looking for work. I remember the nun being very relieved. She told me, 'The school would be a better place without you, Mario.' She went on to say, 'You will only be a vegetable grower, Mario.' At that stage of my young life, I was becoming rebellious. I didn't want to be an altar boy that year and would line up regularly for the cane along with some of my classmates. I remember on colder mornings we would rub our hands with the leaves and berries of a peppercorn tree near the Yenda Catholic School, believing that would take the sting away.

In one incident, the parish priest came to our classroom to tell the pupils he had some disturbing news. The good Father had the habit of saying, 'Right you are,' after someone had finished a sentence or asked a question. It appeared someone had been pinching lemonade from the church hall on a regular basis.

The Father boomed, 'It displeases me to say there are thieves in the school.'

The room went silent, then, quick as a flash, the school wit replied, 'Right you are.' The whole class burst out in laughter. Everyone in the classroom, including the girls, received the cane (or "the cuts" as it was also called) for our rudeness to the good Father.

In another instance, at playtime, most of the pupils would share their lunch with their classmates. On this day, mother had made me custard and jelly in a jar. The boy sitting next to me had a big bunch of Gordo grapes. I liked those grapes and offered him some of my custard and jelly. He ate a portion, but didn't offer me any grapes. I asked him if I could have just a couple of grapes, but he said, 'No,' so I grabbed the lot and ran away eating the whole bunch. He reported me to the nun. When she heard about it, she summoned me to the convent and told the informant to come as well. Thinking I was going to cop the cane in front of him, the smirk he had on his face quickly changed when the nun pointed to a box of apples and made me pick the biggest one, saying, 'If you were so hungry, Mario, you should have asked me.' Then the Sister said to the other person, 'Turn around,' and gave him two cuts across his back, telling him not to be such a mean tittle-tat. I thought the Lord certainly worked his magic in strange ways that day.

Getting back to my first job, at 14 years and 6 months old, I started to make wooden fruit boxes on contract working for Mr Zanatta. It was tedious work, the hours were long, and the work was very noisy. There were about eight of us employed to bang away with a hammer and nails.

From Chump to Champ: With my first job came instructions — hammer the nail into the wood; the quicker you make boxes the more money you make, but be careful. This was told to me by the boss' son. With the first blow of the hammer I belted my thumb and forefinger, and from that discussion I remember wrapping the handkerchief around my thumb. The forefinger was bruised and bled all day. I was more careful for the rest of the day, having to use my third finger and a very sore thumb. Needless to say, I didn't have many boxes on that first day.

I now hold a title that has never been challenged. Making boxes — fastest at making boxes on contract.

Boxes included a softwood, half-bushel box which needed about twenty nails inserted in the wood. They would give us an average-sized box filled with nails about one inch to one-and-a-half inches long, a large scoop resembling a fork with many prongs and much larger, longer teeth, and a hammer with which we would make our wooden boxes. There was also the Bushel Box requiring 32 nails, the Tomato Dump requiring about sixteen nails; and then there was the hardwood Rock melon Crate, which was large and cumbersome requiring 36 nails. There were about eight of us employed; the boss himself would join in, and for a time he was the fastest. The hours were long, boring and tedious, but the money was good. I would sometimes earn £40 a week — a lot of money in those days from 1951 to 1955. Today, that would probably be $1500–$2000, I don't know! A lot!

I will explain how it was done. We would take about six nails from the scoop with our thumb and forefinger in our left hand, then bang away with the hammer in our right hand, inserting three nails into two pieces of softwood, and flip the softwood to the other side. The same thing would be done again. We would then lay the box on its side inserting another four nails, flip it around, insert another four nails and the half Bushel Box was made ready for sale. We put it in a stack behind us, whereupon at the end of the day, the boss would count how many boxes were made. That's how we got paid. After about three months I was to become the fastest in the Yenda, Griffith-Murrumbidgee region.

I matched it with other fast men. Yenda's case makers were faster than Griffith's. One man wanted to put me on at the Griffith Show. I remember bank managers, water bailiffs and others out of town coming to watch me strut my stuff; my bosses acknowledged I had become the fastest. I received offers from the Griffith producers, the Midway Store, Griffith private packing sheds on farms, and a lovely man at Yoogali offering me half his business if I would make boxes for him. On a lighter note, our Leader of the Opposition, Tony Abbott, made a surprise trip into Griffith. He stated how his grandparents owned a five-acre fruit farm at Yenda. I remember the name Abbott well, coming to the packing shed to purchase boxes. So, there we go. Perhaps I have given service to a future Prime Minister's family.

How can I prove I hold the title?

"Fastest Man to Ever Make Wooden Boxes in the Murrumbidgee Irrigation Region" requires proof. I have no trophy. They were not given out in those days. There was no competition except when we were working against one another.

What I do have is word of mouth. There may still be two dozen or more people in Yenda who would remember: a former boss, the man who wanted to put me on at the show, the boss' son, plenty of people in their sixties if they are still alive. If it was to be put on radio or in the papers, I am sure there would be plenty of people from Griffith and Yenda who remember. Apart from that, I know, and also my fellow workers know. I was the best.

Getting back to my first job, one day curiosity got the better of me and I started up the boss' truck. It went right through the back shed and brought the two back doors crashing down. Mr Rosie Zanatta was furious and sacked me on the spot.

I told my mother what had happened and she said, 'Never mind, go back tomorrow with your bike, stay in front of your workplace, make sure you are seen by the two bosses, and then wait and see.' Sure enough, one of the two bosses told Mr Zanatta and he gave me my job back. That was my first lesson in marketing myself.

After I left school, I was still working for Mr Rosie Zanatta. At the time he not only owned a packing and box-making shed, but he also had a fruit run. I was teamed up with a friend called Jake; he had left school six months previously and got a job at Mr Zanatta's.

On this particular expedition, I remember what our first experience of free enterprise was all about. The truck was a *Ford*. The gates were six to seven feet high. I'm not sure, but

I do plainly remember that the cabbages and cauliflowers were stacked much, much higher than the gates.

Our first job was a trip to West Wyalong. We were to sell cabbages to the fruit shops, or so Jake and I thought. Early next morning, there we were knocking on doors at 5.00am with two cabbages on each arm. We somehow had to obtain 4s a cabbage (or better if we could), whilst at the same time keeping barking dogs at bay. I remember my friend commenting at the time, 'It must be good to be a boss,' because Rosie Zanatta never got out of his truck, he just kept driving and told us to hurry up.

I remember we had to have all the houses of West Wyalong covered by 11.00am. We were told we could then go and have lunch, only to find out that because the cabbages weren't all sold, he parked his truck in front of the hotel in West Wyalong until we eventually sold them. This was at about 3.00pm. I sometimes wonder if this was what prompted my friend into going into small business himself shortly after.

I have fond memories of Jake playing lock forward in first grade for Yenda whilst I played at scrum half. It seemed to me he was overly protective. I am still not sure whether it was to score points for Yenda, or to have me fit and ready for the rice and wheat lumping next morning, because by this time Zanatta had sold his business to Eno and Jake Cauduro.

Whilst the transition was taking place, I wasn't sure what was happening and got a job working for the Yenda Producers making boxes on wages. Sometime later, Mr Eno Cauduro came to see me, telling me if I went back and worked for him and his brother there would be work all year round, guaranteed. I could work on contract during the busy fruit season and on wages for the rest of the year.

Whilst I was weighing up my options, the manager of Yenda Producers, Mr Ken Dobson, heard about it and sacked me. I worked for about four years, for firstly Zanatta, then Cauduro Bros, but the constant banging of a hammer against a box gave me migraine headaches. Shortly after, I left to join the railways. After my time in Lithgow, which was about three years, with national service in the same years, I transferred back to Griffith. Steaming up the colourful Blue Mountains through 10 zig-zag tunnels and taking the train through to Bathurst and Orange, one really had to shovel coal to get those huge loads over the mountains. It was hard work and kept us fit.

Griffith was vastly different. The terrain was flat and the work wasn't hard at all. One job was to take the train to the Griffith Producers and wait until they filled it up with produce, which could take up to five hours. To pass the time, we would play table tennis, darts or whatever took our fancy. Another job was to go to a local winery and wait several hours. It gave some of us a chance to do some wine tasting. Mostly, it was sweet sherry.

However, the best job was going to Roto, a township about 300 kilometres south-west of Griffith on the Broken Hill line. It was a three-day journey by train in those days, and we would book off and remain in Roto for the day and night. We only had mosquitoes and flies for company. Quite often, it was agreed the fireman should jump the rattler just past the Olympic swimming pool and go home. The guard sometimes did the same thing.

It all got too much. I was getting fat and lazy and, shortly after, I resigned from the railways to the disappointment of my mother. I found an old exercise book shortly after her passing, which read:

Mario Trainee Engineman (Lith.) Nov 1955
Mario Acting Fireman Lithgow 1956
Mario Appointed Fireman Griffith 1957, I hope.
Mario Acting Driver Griffith 1958, I hope.

My mother did not want me to finish up working in a dead-end job or on farms. She wanted to see me in a good job. Perhaps, in hindsight, I should have remained on the railways and had the railways paid better money at the time, maybe I would have, but $30 a week was hardly enough.

Whilst still in Lithgow, my mother would insist I send her my washing, saying it would give her something to do. My mates told me it was the height of laziness what I was doing, but I don't think so. Maybe they were a little envious that I had such a kind, caring mother.

I believe

My mother and her mother never lost their faith in God. In Yenda the nuns would visit them quite often. A bishop who became a cardinal (it is said third in line for the papacy) visited mother. A parish priest also, in the last years of her life with failing health, administered Holy Communion on a regular basis at her home in Griffith.

The priest would tell me, 'Your mother is a true believer, she believes where even some priests doubt.' That great belief has been passed on to myself.

I believe; because one night I was skylarking off an electric train with one arm hanging off the train railing, my body fully exposed and my right arm outstretched even further. I pulled myself back just in time from the electric steel posts, a yard or two away from the train. It was at night, I was in the army, 19 years old and somewhere near Sydney.

I believe; because in the early 1980s my truck ran out of brakes again. This time it was in the Cullerin Ranges and we were loaded with rock melons for the Sydney markets. I had a mate with me, whose name was Peter Melero, and for 20 kilometres it was all downhill. The truck was going at such a speed I kept it on the wrong side of the road to keep it from rolling over. Strangely, no semi-trailer, car or motorbike was on the stretch of road that night. We got out of the truck, our legs shaking, and praised the Lord for our narrow escape.

I believe; because one day at the Yenda Hotel in the mid-1960s I had an altercation with a man in the main bar. My girlfriend, several of my mates and I were upstairs in a room. After a while, the man went to go home. I spotted him through the window and called out, 'Four eyes.' He called me a few worse words than that. Having a bit of the amber ale inside me and wanting to impress my girlfriend, I took off in pursuit after him.

In the *Valiant* two-door, hard-top sedan I chased him until he let me catch him near a house where two brothers lived. A man, whose name was Squizzy, also witnessed this incident. The man came out of his house firing a semi-automatic. He must have fired about 10 shots into the ground. He came up to me and pointed the gun at my forehead. I thought, *This is it*. My girlfriend leaned her head on my shoulder, not a whimper, not a plea; what a brave girl she was. All I could say to him was, 'Is it worth it? I will die, but you will spend the rest of your life paying for it in jail.' He looked at me for what seemed like an eternity, took the gun away from my forehead and fired another five or six bullets into the ground. I remember him telling me, 'Get out of here, if I ever see you again, I will blow your head off.' To this day, I can't recall ever calling anybody "four eyes" again. My friends back at the Yenda Hotel told me he came from Wollongong and had just been released from jail.

I believe; because of the hard life my mother was forced to lead, both mentally and physically. One of her sisters said to her that because I had no father, I would not grow up right. A brother-in-law told her that when those people go like that, put them away, leave them alone, forget about them (meaning, my father). It must have cut my mother up, knowing he was the one man who could have done something in those early critical years, but my mother soldiered on, believing there would be a better life for her, for her son, for her mother. And life did get better. Mother built a front verandah onto our two-room hut and also a back verandah in 1950. It was better because we could now entertain people who visited us in another room. Our relatives from Victoria could sleep on the front verandah when they visited. I was moved from the attic to the back verandah. I missed our two-roomed hut with the ladder going upstairs to the attic; it was still there, but not quite the same.

I believe; because I was meant to care for my mother. It didn't matter what path I was to take in life's journey: my romances, my fights, my rugby league days, building a transport empire in Griffith, becoming an agent for a plastic bin and pallet hiring business (the plastic bins were to become arguably the biggest in Australia), building a brick agency, a Comet overnight small parcels agency, and a town carrier in Yenda, I became big in boxing promotions and was also a trainer and manager. I had feuds with the NSW railways and then with the truckies of Razorback. For a while, I became a political activist in defence of the growers. And then my foray in fruit farming, working as a bouncer at the Griffith RSL hall, as a table waiter at the Yoogali Club — these were all secondary, just a blowing of the wind. They were all unimportant compared to what my greater goal in life was.

'Look after your mother, son; she has lived only for you, now you must live for her.'

A superior being, far greater than we can ever imagine told me this. That's why He has saved me so many times, I believe.

I believe; because when a crazed 20-year-old attacked me at a buck's party held at the transport terminal, it all went wrong. This big young man smashed a beer bottle and told me he was going to cut my face up. I asked him why, what had I done? He said he had twice asked me for a job and he was refused. He was fuelled on alcohol and kept coming forward, slashing at me. In my attempts to keep away from him, I slipped and took my first cut above the ankle. It was only a matter of time before he got me and he did, in the ribcage. It hurt, but I was able to grab Buddha's arm and kept striking him until he dropped that jagged bottle. I then put a couple of good ones on him and he went to sleep.

Accepting my friends' pats on the back and thanking God for a narrow escape, I thought it was all over, but Buddha woke up and came at me again with the bottle. However, I knocked him out again. When he finally woke up, he stormed off calling me a "mother" something.

The next morning, Buddha came to see me and asked if I would teach him to fight. This was the same young man who, as an eleven-year-old, took his father's car and drove it to Melbourne. It made headlines in the *Area News*. I knew he was brave, his courage just had to be channelled in the right direction. Buddha came and trained under me; it must have been about 1980. He promised he would not attack me again and would only use his fists in the ring. Buddha had three contests and won the lot. He had one on a Grantlee Kieza (journalist) promotion in Griffith and another two at the Yenda Memorial Hall. He left town shortly after his third bout.

I believe; because arguably the biggest brawl ever seen in Griffith was at the Griffith Hotel. Pickers from the Northern Territory were in town to harvest the tomato crop. It was on a Saturday afternoon, probably in January or February 1968. The hotel was packed, people were drinking outside and I remember it being a very hot day. My mates and I were celebrating that my girlfriend had bought me a new jumper, which I was wearing at the hotel, with all that heat. The evening wore on, the shouts got bigger, the beer tasted better and, for whatever reason, I became involved in a dispute with a South Seas Islander. Push came to shove and it was on.

We started inside the hotel. He caught me first and whacked me a good one. I recall he was a good mover and could fight a bit. I gradually started to wear him down. We carried on outside onto the footpath belting each other against cars. His mates were cheering him on. Things turned ugly when I started getting on top, but just to make sure, I picked him up and belted his head against a car bonnet. A big man came over and belted me; Roger and Brian, my friends, bashed him in return. It really started from there. Everyone in the bar seemed to join in, and the fight spilled out onto the roadway. It was the most amazing thing.

The old Griffith Hotel, where my two friends and I jumped off the top balcony, to escape an angry crowd.

People seemed to be fighting each other not really knowing who was on whose side. Through it all, I remember a Spanish man knocking me to the ground. I got up and chased him, and the tomato pickers chased us. I chased him inside what was then known as the Mona Café. He stopped, picked up a large ashtray, and threw it at me. Fortunately, it missed. I remember crash-tackling him and I proceeded to give him what he gave me.

The owner of the Mona Café, I think his name was Calaizis, was trying to keep the crowd out by closing his glass partitioning doors. He told us to make a run for it, out through the kitchen, then jump his back fence whilst he tried to keep them out.

Taking a look at them trying to smash that front door down facing Banna Avenue to get to us, we decided the bravest thing to do was to escape. However, after we leapt over the fence there were tomato pickers in Banna Lane and still in Kooyoo Street.

We had an element of surprise and raced up the back stairs to the top balcony before they realised it was us. We were on the outside patio wondering what to do next when we heard the howling mob racing up the back stairs. That made up our mind for us. We shook hands, looked at each other, then jumped from the top balcony onto Kooyoo Street.

We figured if we could make it to our car, we had some chance of getting out of this with our bodies intact. The car was parked at a service station on the corner of Kooyoo and Yambil Streets where Griffith real estate CVGT now stands. I was hoping upon hope the keys would still be in the car (people left their keys and their doors open those days).

The keys were there, we locked our windows and doors, and I started the car which was a sky-blue 1964 *Holden*. Then a strange thing happened. We looked at one another and decided to go home through Kooyoo Street and not Yambil Street. My friends and I still talk about it today. We drove slowly down Kooyoo Street, watching as they spat and kicked at our car, and turned into Banna Avenue where the mob was on top of the roof and on the bonnet. In front of the Mona Café, I stopped. My friends got out and removed them physically, we went a bit further and it was the same thing. We all took our turn several times getting in and out of the car fighting them off. The crowd seemed surprised by our tactics and hesitated. They weren't frightened, just confused.

We were in the clear; we drove off and went home. The police, I believe, had their hands full that night. The jails were full in Griffith, Yenda and Leeton. How many of them were there? I am positive at least 50, if not more.

My new woollen jumper was a mess; it was covered in blood. I thought getting it dry-cleaned would fix it. However, it came out two sizes smaller and looked nothing like a new jumper. My next move was to go to the menswear store where my fiancée worked at the time. Whilst she was out, I made arrangements with her employer to purchase another one. All was well that ended well, until we broke up and gave back our presents. My ex wanted to know how it was she received such a scruffy jumper when I was walking around with a nice one.

I do believe there is a supreme commander up there somewhere. I do believe He is there for all of us. I also believe we each have a guardian angel that watches over us.

I believe; because it happened in 1969 after I had purchased my beloved little green truck. With the added business, I was able to afford a worker to help me on the farm. His name was Wayne. It was a good arrangement as

Wayne liked the farm and I liked doing the deliveries around the township of Yenda. After work, we would congregate at the Yenda Hotel for a few drinks. This particular night we had stayed longer than normal and it was quite dark when we decided to go home. I lived in Griffith. I was taking my friend home; not looking where I was driving and chatting away, when my car hit the nature strip on the right-hand side of Main Avenue, Yenda. The car veered out of control and headed straight for Suman's Engineering Factory on the left of the road.

The car hit a fence and completely uprooted the black corrugated post out of the ground. The post went under the car and came up through the floorboards between Wayne and myself. Had that post gone six inches either to the left or right it could have been curtains for one of us.

That, dear reader, is why I believe in guardian angels.

Somewhere in the early 1990s, I acted and sang in a play called *Down Memory Lane*, at the Presbyterian Hall. It played for three nights and was a sellout. I felt good about that, I felt clean, I was among Christian people. I felt it was me, the real me.

Once, at a Full Gospel Businessman's dinner, I was asked to sing and give my testimony. I sang *One Day At A Time*, with the words fighting and shoving and crowding my mind. It seemed appropriate for the time.

My testimony was based on religion and why I believed in the creator, what He had done for me up to that point of time. One of the issues I mentioned was a battle I was having coping with my extremely bad back, a legacy left to me (probably) from rugby league days, hard work, or the rough life I had led.

I tried chiropractors, physiotherapists, and acupuncture. My doctor had me in hospital for two weeks on lead weights, all to no avail. I remember it quite well; it was a point of time in my life when both my mother and I were depressed. I knew quite well what was wrong with my mother — she had told a friend who told me. My mother felt doomed to never have a grandchild and this led me to say to her, 'Mother, if I am to get married, I must leave home and live by myself for a while.' At the moment, people probably think I don't want to be married. They are probably saying I'm a mother's boy, that I am tied to my mother's apron strings.

However, it wasn't a good move. I lived in a flat by myself where mother would come and visit me. It was at this point of time I developed the extremely bad back. I was deeply involved in boxing at the time: training, promoting and managing. Fighting was good for the soul, but hard on the body and the hip pocket. My first problem with my back was walking across the street in Banna Avenue, sometime in 1980. I seemed to simply stiffen up, I couldn't move, I couldn't walk, I stayed in the centre of the roadway for a time blocking the traffic until I was helped across the road. Then later, whilst training a boxer for an upcoming middleweight title attempt, I was jogging and doing sprints with him at the Jubilee Sports Oval when my back went again. It was as if part of my spine had dropped.

I stood there not being able to move; I had to be helped into my car. The boxer took me home. I lay in my bed for several days not being able to move, and when I did it was painful.

At that time, with a transport business and a brick business, working as a boxing trainer, manager and promoter, I somehow found time to become a member of the Full Gospel Businessmen's Dinners. It was at one of these meetings that I came in contact with Bishop Malingo from South Africa. It was said he had mystical powers and could cure the sick. At one such religious meeting, people would line up to be cured. The Bishop would pray over them one at a time and tap them on the forehead, whereupon they would presumably faint and on waking up they would be cured. It was my turn. The Bishop prayed over me and looked into my eyes. His eyes seemed to have a magnetic glow about them; it was as if I was being hypnotised. He tapped me on the forehead, but I wouldn't go down or faint, I wasn't going to take a dive for anyone, not even a Bishop. However, my back did feel better. I wonder whether it was divine intervention or the good physiotherapist I had recently found. Only God knows for sure.

Troubled times

My business collapsed, my semi-trailer tipped over barely 100 yards from my workplace, I was arrested for assault, and then I was questioned over parking my car on the lawn during a funeral and questioned over backing my car into another car.

My life had been a colourful one. I was an onlooker, then a participant, in one of the biggest brawls ever seen in Griffith. I was involved in a fight to the death on Griffith's Scenic Hill. In business, I took on the NSW Railways during the great train strikes, then again took on the truckies during Razorback. I fought for my life against a crazed man called Buddha. I also, for a time, became a political activist in defence of the growers of Griffith. I started businesses in Griffith, such as town carrier, Comet overnight agent, Mario's Beautiful Bricks, and a fruit and vegetable transport business, which became arguably the biggest in NSW outside Sydney. I also started a pallet-hiring company. All these businesses still operate, under other names perhaps, but the jobs and trades are still there. I am proud of what I achieved. I suppose, in a way, I became a celebrity by default. I'm sure my mother thought so, though doesn't every mother think her son is a celebrity?

Grandfather

Poor, unfortunate grandad had to do it the hard way. How he purchased the five-acre farm block of Farm 737 Yenda is unclear. Perhaps his son, Giovanni, loaned (or gave) him the money. Whatever the situation was, Uncle John could not get along with his father. Grandad wanted John to give the farm at Beelbangera to him, as was the Calabrese custom of that era. Or perhaps it was just grandad's custom.

There is a story told by some of the older Calabrese that Giovanni Agostino, because he could not get along with his father, went and lived with the hermit on the hill for three months. Perhaps Grandad was jealous of his son's effort. Giovanni Agostino, who worked in the coalmines of Moss Vale and the fruit farms of Griffith, saved his money and got his entire family out from Italy to Australia. It has already been mentioned what happened to my grandfather. However, I should add that after the incident with the toilet can, he asked the police to put him into a mental asylum.

A very old passport photo taken of my grandfather in 1928

My mother told me he went home and threw a stone into a neighbour's window; he then went back to the police telling them what he had done, demanding that they put him into the mental hospital. This they did. This incident happened in 1941 when I was four years old. Nine years later, my mother, her youngest sister and I went to Kenmore hospital at Goulburn and took grandad home. I was glad as I thought that my dad and my uncles would be next, but it was not to be.

Grandad tried hard, he grew his vegetables and tried to sell them the best he could.

When a girl marries

There is one thing grandad got right, which was to marry off his daughters to the right people. He married his eldest daughter Anna to Frank Jack Pompeani in June 1931, three months after they had landed in Australia. She was 22 years old. Grandad married off his next daughter, Theresa, to Giovanni Bellicanta. She was married in July 1933 at the age of 17. Theresa was born on 30 December 1916.

In 1934, my dad, Paolo Lorenzo Guerra, married my mother, Caterina Agostino, on 1 December 1934. My mother was born on the 8 June 1919, making her not quite 16.

In 1936, Maria Rosa Agostino married Don Moretto on 16 August 1936. Maria was born in November 1921, making her 15 years old.

In 1945, Carmela Agostino married Lorenzo Cunial on 5 February 1945. Carmela was born on 22 June 1924; she was 21 years old.

How well I remember the Italian men courting Carmela. They came with respect to our hut in Yenda, five or six at a time, with our hut and attic always spotlessly clean. The men would gather around our table, play poker and other card games. The prize money was matchsticks. I remember grandmother and her two daughters thoroughly enjoying themselves.

It was one windy, rainy night when our kerosene lamp blew out. I remember the wind was very strong. When they eventually got the lamp going and several candles, the table was covered in grass seeds, leaves and dust that had obviously come through the top of the roof.

Grandfather may have been dirt-poor but he built a sturdy house and raised well-mannered daughters, who were all attractive as the photo shows. In that era, Northern and Southern Italians stayed away from each other. However, this didn't stop the Northern Italians from wooing and winning Guiseppe Agostino's four daughters. With one daughter married to a man from the Abruzzi region of Ripa (somewhere between the middle and southern part of

Italy), grandfather proved he had his family's best interests at heart by working hard on his block of land, building a sturdy house for those times and marrying his daughters off to good men. What a pity those good men couldn't help grandfather in his time of need, what a pity grandfather's daughters couldn't help their father, their mother, or their sister in their great hour of need. Things had been terribly hard but the war was over. Some of my mother's sisters were buying farms and becoming affluent. It's a great pity nothing was done.

Once, when my mother's youngest sister was married and the wedding was over, she spent her honeymoon on a farm on Gordon Road, Yenda. It must have been about 10 kilometres farther from where she lived in Barracks Road. My mother was very excited; she was going to prepare her sister a surprise wedding breakfast. Mother woke me up very early and together we set off on our bikes with the breakfast all prepared neatly on hot plates, wrapped in large white serviettes. Making a knot, we carried two each on our handlebars.

As I remember, the road was still all gravel. I recall we had to ride carefully so as not to receive a puncture or spill the breakfast. At the young age of eight, I thought what a lot of trouble mother had gone to. That was my mother; she enjoyed doing good things for other people, especially her sisters.

We made it to the neat-looking, red, weatherboard house on Rossetto's farm; the groom and the bride were still in bed. They looked a little surprised, but happy that mother had gone to so much trouble for them.

Another time, when I was in my twenties, mother received a letter that some relatives of ours from Melbourne would like to come and visit. My mother was very excited and started preparing beds for them to sleep and also preparing and cooking food. She told her sisters, who seemed bemused that mother was going to so much trouble. They came in carloads. As it turned out, they weren't really our cousins and had come to Yenda to get in some pig shooting. After being told they were at least 200 kilometres away from the pigs, they asked if I could accompany them on a pig hunt. They stayed the night and we set off next morning, my mother and grandmother not quite knowing what to make of it all. We arrived in West Burrabogie in the township of Hay that morning, whereupon they commenced shooting at everything they saw. They were armed with shotguns and wore gumboots that reached right up their legs, the same type my mother would use when she washed carrots. They were terrible hunters, getting only 14 tiger snakes, one rabbit, a porcupine and then, very late in the evening, a pig. However, the pig wasn't a big one, it wasn't dangerous and it was run down. The snakes were something else; there were so many of them. I was glad to get out of that place. I have never been back.

We arrived home at about 11.00pm. Our guests stayed the night and left next morning with the pig in a crate. We never heard from them again. My dear mother, forever gullible, was always trusting. She was taken advantage of many times in her lifetime by people who should have known better.

Fruit farming days: It was 1963 and my case-making days

were numbered. I now had to compete against a machine, which could make two boxes to my one.

My only chance was that, since it was a machine, it would break down quite often. However, the noise was deafening, I got tinnitus in my right ear. It is said constant loud noise is what causes it. I still have it, as there is no cure. Perhaps eight years of banging hammer against nail caused it.

It was time to move on, but I didn't know where. I seriously considered moving to Sydney to try my luck when a friend mentioned to me the opportunity of a lifetime. He said, 'You can work for this farmer for a year on wages then lease it off him.' My mother wasn't happy. She disliked fruit farms and we still had our five-acre block full of vegetables to contend with.

However, I must say the seven years I spent on that farm made me happy. My first year working for myself in 1964 was very profitable, enabling us to purchase a house in Griffith. The work consisted of five months pruning the peaches on top of a horse and trailer and the rest of the year preparing the land: fertilising, watering and spraying the peach trees.

We had about six weeks to pick the peaches and get them to the cannery. This would be done in two ways: by using a truck the farmer had loaned me, or with a horse and trailer. We would take the peaches into the depot at the Yenda Producers about eight kilometres away where the semi-trailer would take them to the Leeton cannery.

The farmer's wife matched me at picking and pruning the peaches. She worked for me on wages and assisted greatly in finding labour during the critical six-weeks, peach-picking period. She found about a dozen ladies, with some coming from Griffith. They could all work as hard as any man and the best part was the morning and afternoon teas brought to us by the farmer's wife. I have read with interest about the feats of the Land Army Girls during the war years and believe everything written about them after watching those peach-picking ladies. They also chipped and weeded rock melons, and shook and picked prunes, which could be back-breaking work.

My mother and grandmother also helped after finishing work at the hospital. The women all had great respect for mother and would call her Cathy or Cath. Two other men and I would do the harder work with one man named Squizzy requesting if he could work down the other end of the paddock. When we asked him why, Mr Squizzy would say, 'Because the women pick on me. It's always "Squizzy do this, Squizzy do that or don't do this and don't do that".' I think he liked all the attention the ladies gave him, though. Another thing I remember about those born-again Land Army Girls: they were always smiling, they were always neat and tidy, and they would sometimes wear lipstick.

I spent seven years on that farm. The first year I worked on wages for the owner. It was a large farm of about 63 acres; it had mostly peaches, but also about 13 acres of prunes and about four acres of apples, with vacant land. Until then, I had spent my life helping my mother's uncles chip or weed grass from the growing vegetables, before school, after school and on weekends. It was a good foundation and taught me the value of work. Until then, I hadn't known much about fruit trees, except how to pick the fruit and grapes off the trees. The year I spent working the fruit farm on wages was a good experience in my foray of working for myself.

It was 1964. At 28 years I had finally become my own boss and I was to come to terms with nature, with the elements, and with the insects. I learned the right time to irrigate the peaches. I was given half the farm: about 23 acres of peaches, three acres of prunes and four acres of vacant land to grow vegetables. I enjoyed my time on the farm, having two very good years, two bad years and two ordinary years.

However, I never really liked farming. For instance, I would have to hold a placard over my head and signal a crop sprayer to fly in and spray the peach trees with a powerful insecticide because of a new type of insect which had attacked the peaches. I must have been sprayed from the top of my head to the bottom of my toes every time I moved the placard from one row of peaches to the next.

We didn't seem to understand how dangerous insecticides could be in that era. A lot of people became sick, and some died. It was thought insecticides had something to do with it. I recall an engineer who would quite happily get inside the spray vats and weld whatever needed fixing. He passed away in the time I leased the fruit farm. Another engineer from Yenda passed away several years earlier. It was enough to convince me I should move on.

Cops: My dealings with the police of Yenda and Griffith have been hot and cold. I first came into contact with the police when I lived in Yenda and I was only a youth in my early teenage years. I played with Sergeant Reeve's sons almost daily and we kept in contact through the 1970s and 1980s. However, about 1958, my mate Tony and I rocked out of the Yenda hotel a bit under the weather. My mate dared me to drive through the Yenda park. Not wanting to refuse a dare, I went for it. It was a large park, whilst we made it to the other side we were being watched by an interested spectator. It was Constable Bugden of Yenda. He caught me at the public school. I was taken back to the police station and charged. He said, 'I told you not to hang around with that Dole bloke.' I decided to go to church that night and pray to God to forgive me of my sin, as I did not want mum to find out. I noticed Constable Bugden also was attending mass, probably praying that I should not be forgiven me for my sin. When mass finished, and I was driving home from the church grounds, something made me turn left into Barracks Road and not right. A truck collided with the back of my car. The driver had been rushing his pregnant wife to Griffith District Hospital, as her baby was due. Constable Bugden was quickly on the scene and wanted me charged, but my friends wanted no part of it, they just wanted to get to the hospital. Constable Bugden took them in the police car. The baby was born healthy. Not to be outdone, the constable visited my workplace the next afternoon, advising me I needed to help him measure the distance where I drove my car across the park — this was watched by interested drinkers at the Yenda Hotel. Not wanting my mother to find out, I asked the friendly reporter if he would keep the court hearing out of his paper. 'Sure,' he replied, 'it was not a problem.' However,

I forgot that Griffith had two papers, probably owned by the same company. My mother found out and Yenda had a good laugh, with some of my friends saying the council was going to paint the roads green so I could stay on the road, referring, I suppose, to the green lawn of the park. I managed to keep out of trouble until the mid-1960s. It happened at night time when two Aussies with Italian names were smashing one another in front of the Yenda Hotel. They were arrested and locked up in the Yenda jail. Having too much of the amber ale inside me, I decided to get my mate out of the lockup. Armed with a rope, I climbed up the water spout at the back of the rather high-bricked Yenda lockup. Reaching the top, I yelled out, 'Don't worry, Tony, I will get you out.' A surprised Tony replied, 'Righto.' However, I was confronted with a glassed rooftop. For some reason I thought that the top of the bricked wall was open air. While working out what to do next and chatting with my friend, a person walked out of the house next door to the jail, saying someone was trying to break into jail. I dropped to the ground quickly and ran away, but the policeman wasn't far behind. He grabbed Tony's brother, Tim, who was in the vicinity, ordering him to use the spotlight to catch the character.

The police and Tim chased me all over Yenda; wherever I ran, that spotlight wasn't far behind. I jumped over fences and through the back yards of houses. I seemed to be forever running from that spotlight. I hid in the toilet at the back of the Yenda bank, but the light was not far behind me. I got out of there and made it to Girdlers' hay shed which was not far from the main street. That is where I stayed for several hours. I finally made it to Tony and Tim's parents' residence and informed them of what had happened and went to sleep under one of the beds.

The next morning a policeman visited me at the fruit farm I worked on at the time, it was about 11.00am. The officer said to me, 'You know, Mario, a funny thing happened last night. Someone tried to break into the lockup. I have heard of people trying to break out, but never of anyone trying to break in. I tell you what I will do. I will nab you for fighting and swearing. That will only cost you $72 and I will forget the other incident because you are only going to deny it.' 'But, sir,' I replied. 'Tut tut,' said the lawman and pointed a stern finger at me. I didn't push my luck and left it at that.

One night in the early 1970s, I came across a young cop fending off five rough-looking types in front of the Victoria Hotel in Griffith. Constable Falcon was handling himself pretty well. I raced in and helped Ron Falcon so that the odds were even, causing the thugs to run away. We remain friends to this day.

Sometime in the 1980s an incident happened at Ziggy's Restaurant and Night Club in Griffith. Located down the stairs opposite the La Scala Restaurant, a little bloke had too much to drink and was ordered out. He was irate and said he was coming back to blow all the wogs away. I had a few drinks myself and decided to leave in case he did. The coast seemed clear as I drove off in my *Toyota Supra*. After a kilometre or two, I noticed a police car following me. I tried to out-speed them, but they were getting closer. I drove into a driveway and stopped the car. Running through someone's house I attempted to jump the high fence. I slipped and the police caught up with me. I struggled with the three of them saying, 'Don't shoot, don't shoot!' I remember one of them saying, 'Behave yourself, Mario, we are not going to shoot you. I then explained about the little man at Ziggy's who was going to shoot all the *wogs*, including me, and I thought they were him. My ruse didn't work and I was put on the breathalyzer. I went over the limit and was taken to the police station. It must have been an hour later, and I was tested again and this time was just under the limit, with one of the police saying, 'Thank you, Mr Guerra, for the donation you gave to the Police Boys Club recently.'

Another time, a truck needed to be taken to Sydney loaded with produce for the markets. At the time I had no licence, so I obtained the services of a worker and together we went to Sydney. We unloaded the produce, and loaded another load to go back to Griffith. Everything was going fine until the driver, Johnny Jeffery, needed a break at Yass. I took over using Johnny Jeffery's licence, making sure I drove very carefully, thinking I would be safe. However, at about Harden-Murrumburrah, a policeman drove alongside and signalled for me to pull over. On getting out, the constable asked me what my name was. I replied, 'Johnny Jeffery.' He looked long and hard at me saying, 'You don't look like no Johnny Jeffery.' He then asked for my licence. I thought, *My goose is cooked, I'm gone*. The real Johnny Jeffery, on hearing his name, looked out of his bunk and the policeman ordered him out.

There we were, two Johnny Jefferys with one licence. I

explained what had happened. He was a good cop as he told the real Johnny Jeffery to drive back to Griffith. He let me off with a warning.

I think in all of us is the desire to become a cop, catch the bad guys and help the good guys.

Big man from Vietnam in fight to the death

It was 1961. It started, I believe, when I was working as a waiter at the Yoogali Club. It was about midnight on Saturday night and there was a commotion in the foyer. I noticed a big man standing over another man who had been knocked down, who was saying, 'Just wait until I get up, I will knock you out.' His nickname was Big Tiny, because he had the habit of taking on men much bigger than himself. However, he was under the weather and was stopped before he could go on with it. The big man challenged everyone else who were watching to fight him. This invitation was accepted by a friend of mine, named Teddy Scobie. It was agreed they would fight at the Griffith Ex-Servicemen's Oval. It must have been about 12.30am on Sunday morning.

People left the club to watch, with the cars forming a circle. We put our lights on so the gladiators could see themselves. Teddy had had a bit to drink and wasn't getting the best of it; the further it went the worse it got for Scobie. The big man said, 'Who wants it next?' I remember saying, 'I do.' He had a weakness; I capitalised on it. His face was covered in blood and he said he had enough. I remember he complained he had two fights previously and wanted to fight me again.

About a month later, I was challenged. I had to meet him at the Griffith Hotel at 5.00pm to make arrangements where to fight. It was agreed we would go up Scenic Hill to one of the lookouts. I remember wanting to get it over with quickly, as I had an engagement party to attend.

The fight was almost an exact replica of the first one, except it went on for longer. His face was again covered in blood; I again exploited his weakness; he once again said he had enough. The only difference was this time I received a small nick on my right eye. The big man said he was going to Vietnam to fight for his country and would challenge me when he came back. At the time, he could have been about 19. I was 24 years old. In all my disagreements and street fights, I cannot recall ever throwing the first blow or wanting to fight someone, or wanting to hate someone. I have had about 60 street fights that I can remember; all of them to defend my honour. What I went through with redneck thugs during my school days and early teenage years scarred me forever.

About two years later, I was still working at the Yoogali Club. I recall there was a midnight-to-dawn dance being held at Hanwood Hall, a village about 10 kilometres out of Griffith. I decided to go after finishing work at 1.00am. The big man was back from Vietnam and with his mates and it wasn't long before I was picked on. I tried to talk my way out of it, but the big man wouldn't have any part of it, wanting to fight me outside in the hall right away. It must have been about 2.00am or 3.00am. I told him and his mates I had been working all night and needed two hours' rest to prepare myself.

At 6.00am, my friend, Big Tiny, woke me at my mother's place. It was time. We ventured to Scenic Hill to the same place we had fought two years ago. It was winter, it was very cold, and quite a large crowd had gathered. They had built a large fire; it was more like a bonfire. It was so cold we stood around warming ourselves until about 7.00am when it was daylight and we could actually see ourselves.

I recall the big man saying, 'Let's go, Mario, we fight to the death this time, I'm sick of it.' And a fight to the death it was ... almost!

The big man came out fast, throwing his haymakers from everywhere. He landed quite a few. This time he looked fitter, stronger; he had a crazy look in his eyes as if he wanted to kill me. The last two times we met, I let him punch himself out. It wasn't happening this time. I decided I would go with him; I would dart in with three or four punches to his face, mostly on his mouth and teeth, then move out quickly. The battle went on for a long time. The pattern of the fight now was who could take the most punishment. He was strong, but I was fit. I would dart in with quick punches whilst he would bullock me, hoping to land his big ones. We fought inside a closed enclosure of chains, which resembled a boxing ring, except the chains and the posts were lower. My punches aimed for his eyes and eyebrows. I was fit, very fit; I had always kept myself that way. One of his eyes was almost closed; also, I remember his other eye was glazed. He was mine; he was ready for the kill. His face was a bloody mess, his lips were cracked and swollen and he was staggering towards the chain fence. I kept it up. He was somewhere close to the steel post; he couldn't raise his hands; he was gone. He knew it, I knew it, the crowd knew it. There was a referee in attendance for this "fight to the death". I remember saying to the ref, 'He's had enough.' The referee agreed and stepped in, and it was over.

The referee, Ron Jones, was a big man himself. He was a successful first-grade soccer coach for Hanwood and the ideal person to have in such a hate-filled contest. The hate came from some of the man's mates and the big man himself. I heard the words, 'Give it to the *spag*,' but I can't hate and I haven't got the killer instinct that's necessary if you want to reach the top in the boxing world or street fighting.

My fists were a mess, my hands were swollen; they were bloody. To this day, every one of my knuckles is scarred and almost every one of my top index knuckles are marked, as testimony to the struggle that happened on Scenic Hill on that almost fateful morning. I was told the fight went for 45 minutes and it was thought my opponent should go to hospital. However, because the police may have taken more than a passing interest in the matter, it was decided that Jeff and his mates should come to my mother's place. Mother prepared coffee, whilst the man and I washed the blood off our faces and bodies. We all got on well and the amber ale started flowing. I can remember the man asking me to teach him to fight. I replied, 'No way, you can fight well enough.' He had just given me the hardest fight, a fight that could have cost me my life, or his.

Through writing this book, I have found the Kirkmans lived not far away from dad and mother at Beelbangera. It may well have been that my dad and the man's dad knew each other, given that dad was friends with the Langmans and Mr Davis. Had mother known where they were and had she been able to speak to them, I'm sure they would have done something. They would have only had to say to the authorities, 'He's alright mate, we'll look after him.' This, of course, is conjecture.

Going back to Sunday morning 1962, after our fight, the beer and the yarns were still flowing well into the morning and into early afternoon. I left mother's house at 2.00pm to go to Yenda and prepare to play first grade football against Narrandera at Wade Park. We lost the game 13-9, but I won the Best and Fairest award. I had been running on steam, the adrenalin had been working overtime; it's amazing what a sportsman can do when he is super fit.

In all contests in the ring, including four tent fights, I had always been in good shape, except for two occasions: the one against Johnny McManus, when I entered the ring suffering from a hangover, and the one against David Clarke at Balmain Leagues in 1966, when Joey Thompson and I had to lose weight on the eve of the fight. I had to lose three pounds. I remember coming out of that sauna at 9 st. 13 lbs. I had lost 4 lbs. in a matter of hours. I remember

Tommy Colteaux, a great middleweight of an earlier era, rubbing me down. I remember Harden's Bernie McGrath vs. Hans Wagner, and I remember watching Sammy Calabrese and Joey Thompson winning their fights. I also remember David Clarke giving me a hiding for two rounds. Something was wrong. I could hardly hold my hands up; it wasn't me. I was fighting like a big girl.

I was dehydrated both mentally and physically. My trainer, Lyall Jones, told me I had to knock him out in the next round or lose the fight. I gave it all I had; my opponent was tiring. I had him in the corner, but it wasn't enough; David Clarke was announced the winner on points. In his next bout, he fought Keith Skuse, Australian Light Welterweight Champion, for the right to represent his country at the Commonwealth Games held in Montreal, Canada. Clarke lost on points. It was 1972 and I was 35 years old. I remember Constable Ken Donk Hodges was in attendance. He looked sad for me, saying I was only a shadow of what I had been 12 years ago. Ken Hodges promoted the contest with Teddy Scobie, in a main event held at Griffith's Rio Theatre. It was a promoter's dream. The Rio Stadium was packed. I was 11 st. for that contest, a stone heavier than the one I had recently been defeated in. Eleven stone was my right weight. Even though I was short for a light middleweight, I was strong. I was to have one more contest.

Under Lyall Jones, I was matched against aboriginal welterweight Brian Williams from Wilcannia. The contest was fought at Ivanhoe. Williams was a good fighter; he had the same walk-up style as Clarke, and he came out fast. I dropped him for an eight-count in the first round; he did the same to me in the second round. Coming out for the last round, I was very fit and tried to stop him. The fight went the distance and I received the decision.

I drifted out of boxing after that until I visited the Texan Tavern one night. The nightclub was in the heart of Griffith in Banna Avenue, owned by a man named Aussie Bob. It was a popular place and seemed to be packed every night of the week. On this particular night, a big man came up to me and said, 'Hold this beer for me, Mario.' I already had my hand around one beer and obliged by holding his. That's when he cracked a beautiful punch on my chin. The Texan Tavern was built underground. To get in you had to walk down a long line of stairs and to get out was the same.

The big man was a giant, nicknamed The Bear. He raced up the stairs onto the main street. I went in pursuit after him and the crowd left the nightclub to watch the spectacle. It was in the main street. The man called The Bear was there waiting for me. He simply picked me up, threw me to the ground, and appeared to be enjoying himself choking me. A policeman appeared and told us both to go home. I was humiliated. I started up my little red *Subaru* and went after The Bear. It is said I chased him on the footpath, on the nature strip and between the trees. He would just duck behind another tree and laugh.

All was well until we met at the Griffith Ex-Servicemen's Club the following Saturday. This time I was called White Feather. It was on again. However, as it was at the club, we were broken up. I challenged The Bear to meet me at the

Police Boys' Club for a wager of $1000, with the bout to be fought over six rounds with gloves on the following Monday. Previously, I had watched The Bear take on three men in a hotel brawl at the Victoria Hotel. He handled them well. One man jumped on his back but The Bear was too strong for them that day. I had also sparred several times with his brother, a Riverina light heavyweight champion, so I knew what I was in for if I was to win the $1000 wager. The bout was to be refereed by a former policeman called Geoff Foster. When I arrived at the Police Boys' Club on the Monday, there seemed to be a lot of spectators there. The Bear was waiting for me inside the ring. I smelt alcohol on him, he must have been confident

I recall in the first couple of rounds, we just stood there trading blows. The Bear was dirty. I would get him on the ropes, where he would rub the glove laces over my face. He hit me on top of my head, he hit me at the back of my head, he hit me all over my head, he hit me all over my body, he hit me in my groin. I recall I had to change my tactics, so for the next two rounds I made The Bear chase me. I would duck his punches and would weave myself out of trouble. It was the fifth round, and I sensed The Bear was tiring. I punished him for it. I gave it all I had trying to stop him, but he was strong. At the end of the fifth round, I was so tired my corner threw a bucket of water over me, saying, 'You only have to stand up to win, Punchy.'

We came out for the last round. The Bear was tired, the water had revived me, and I won the last round. Geoff Foster crowned me winner. I was very pleased, as once more I had defended my honour. I had just defeated The Bear. It wasn't Marquis of Queensbury; it was a bar room brawl. If it was fought under boxing rules, it would not have gone past one round. It took a couple of minutes to wash the water away from the corner of the ring, giving us both a welcome respite. We made friends. The Bear invited me over for a beer at the Victoria Hotel where he said, 'You are not getting your $1000, I haven't got it.' I told him I didn't care: I won; he lost; that's all that mattered. The last I heard of Bear he was a barman in Albury.

The reason I entered the boxing ring at all was because of what happened in Yenda during my school days. During my teenage years and beyond I had to conquer my fear of being scared of being beaten. Fifteen bouts in the ring including four in the tents and an unofficial fight at the Police Boys' Club — not much by professional or amateur standards, but it gave me what I needed to know: whether I won or lost, I wasn't afraid.

From my first bout in the army, I became extremely confident. Also, being told by top fight trainers, Bernie Hall, Lyall Jones and Stan Brennick, that I could make it all the way to the top, was sweet music to my ears. Likewise, I was told by two great internationals that I could have played for my country had I gone to Sydney or even Wagga. Hearing those words was like manna from heaven. Being told I played for the wrong club saddened me. Try as I might, I could never be accepted as a real Aussie by the rednecks in Yenda.

I did what I had to do: fight them on the streets of Griffith and Yenda and gain their respect. I can remember about 60 street fights, including non-racist ones. A name that stands out is George Manera. We were playing bocce, which is an Italian game similar to lawn bowls, at a sly grog shop in Bilbul. I was on George's side. I couldn't play bowls for nuts. We were losing; George lost his temper, and he cracked a bocce ball over my head. I retaliated and put one on his head. We fought on until we were tired and had enough. Spectators said it was a draw.

About three years later at an open-air concert held in Yenda in front of the Catholic School, my big cousin and I had a half empty bottle of beer. There was a man there whose nickname was Piggy and he was making a nuisance of himself. It was deemed by the hierarchy he should drink our holy urine (according to the law of my big cousin and me). We went looking for Mr Piggy among the big crowd watching the concert. We couldn't find him, but George Manera found us. I remember George was with his new girlfriend. When he approached us, he said, 'Mate, I'll have a beer.'

My big cousin gave George the bottle. I tried to stop him, but it was too late, George must have drunk about a quarter of the bottle when he realised. George let out an almighty roar and yelled, 'Guerra.' I tried to explain it wasn't meant to go that way; it was meant for Piggy. George wouldn't listen and cracked a big punch under my eye. What did I do? What could I do? I had to fight. As I was trying to keep him away from me, I wondered why it was always me and never my big cousin. We fought on, we crashed through the good Sisters of Saint Joseph's tin fence and we fought on the woodpile. By this time the concert was called off as the people had come to watch us fight. We fought under the peppercorn tree where years earlier George and I would rub our hands with peppercorn when we knew we were going to get the cane.

I remember wrestling on the ground when an uncle said, 'Give it to him, Mario.' George replied, 'No barracking.' We fought on and wrestled until we had enough. Who won? It was a draw. I recall my mother giving me a tongue-lashing for an hour or two. We met the next day after work at the Yenda Hotel and we had a laugh and a few beers together to pass the time.

Once a year in Yenda, the ones who had the most fights would win the Best and Fairest Award. In the club were the two Galluppi brothers, my big cousin, George and I. It should be remembered Yenda had one hotel and apart from rugby league and cricket, there wasn't much to do. It had a tennis club, a golf club and a Diggers' Club. Once the picture theatre closed, the hotel and the R.S.L. Club became more inviting. We also had what we in the club called a "Biff A Bikie" week. Once a year, we would go to Griffith looking for motorbike riders. This all happened in the 1960s. We were young, bored and silly. We worked hard on the farms, but, without a girlfriend, Yenda could be a lonely place. I do remember in the 1970s I lost my way. Drink was starting to become a problem. I seemingly had a chip on my shoulder over dad and other things. I became argumentative in the hotels and clubs and, subsequently, I was barred from every club and hotel in Yenda and Griffith. Even the Whitton

Hotel barred my big cousin and me. The only two clubs that hadn't barred me were the Griffith Golf Club and the Jondaryan Club. That was because I never went there!

More about dad

Apart from my father entering an obstacle course at the Griffith Showground, sneaking food and water to the hermit on the hill, and his strongman feats whilst working at a Hanwood winery, I knew little else about him.

Mother told me dad had a beautiful singing voice. She said he was an extremely hard worker and could gulp an apple in half in one bite. My father loved to sing to mother the Bersaglieri song and she, in turn, passed it on to me.

The song goes like this, firstly in Italian:
"Marcha, marcha, marcha le bersaglieri,

Si accende la fiamma la fiamma dell amore-
si accende la fiamma la fiamma dell amore.
Quando ved un bersaglieri pasar
E quando vedo, un bersaglieri batter di gioya, il coure, mi sento,
le gambe mie sento tremar, un bersalyiere mi voqlio sposar.
O bella morettina Italia longassai, il bersaglieri cammina.
Manon si stanca mai, e camina il bersaglieri, con tanto allegramento
Camina il bensaglieri, un bersaglieri mi voglio sposar."

Now in English:

"March on, march on, march on, my soldier,
The flame is burning, is burning in my heart-
the flame is burning, is burning in my heart.
Every time I see, my soldier
and when I see him, oh, my beloved,
beating with joy, my heart I hear,
Oh, my legs, I feel them tremble,
Beloved soldier I want to marry.
Oh, beautiful brown eyes, Italy is very long,
Oh, my beloved soldier becomes even more strong.
March on Italian soldier, with much energy,
March on beloved soldier, you are the one I must marry."

[The words in English have been changed slightly.]

I would sing this song quite often when my mother requested. I sang it to her at a surprise 80th birthday party held in her honour. Most of the Guerras from Victoria made the trip, which was pleasing to my mother.

My story has also taken me to Mr Bob Fanshaw's farm at Beelbangera, where in 1934 my father, living next door, asked could he have a loan of a horse to go to the Sacred Heart Church and make arrangements for his forthcoming wedding to my mother, then Caterina Agostino.

Apparently, as the story goes, dad was legged onto a half-broken-in bolter, aptly named Phar Lap. Dad was legged on; the horse took off and dad was not able to stop the horse at the Sacred Heart Church. The horse just kept going right on past the church and ended up taking dad right back to Mr Fanshaw's farm. Dad got off, saying, 'Him no stop, him no stop.' Dad's broken English may have appeared funny at the time, but was to become deadly serious four years later.

Another story fondly told about dad was when he had just

arrived from Victoria, where he had finished working on a dairy farm with his brother Peter and was introduced to picking peaches. The first thing dad did was to put the peach-picking halter back-to-front on his back and started picking, then throwing the peaches over his back and into the halter.

Dad, it is said, was the first man to plant tomatoes in the Griffith district (as told to me by a lady who is the sister of my mother's bridesmaid). The lady is the late Peter Saggin's sister and she married Louie Bertoldo, mother of Len.

My poem, dedicated to Paul Lorenzo Guerra:

"A migrant man from Italy,
Paul Lorenzo Guerra was his name,
could not speak a word of English,
but 'tis said he was so game,
entering a three-mile race
at the Griffith Show, I'm told,
leaving the others far behind;
they all but caught a cold.

"A test of strength was given he
at a winery one day,
a heavy metal wheel
to be put upon the dray.
With all his strength he mustered,
one, two and three to see,
he performed the amazing feat
at that McWilliam Winery.
"A job at picking peaches

his next work was to be,
his picking bag put on back-to-front,
he picked peaches eagerly.
A fellow worker did tell Paul,
'You are working much too fast.
At the rate that you are going
our job, it will not last.'

"Paul Guerra was a strong man,
of that there is no doubt,
the photos in my story
show what he was all about.
He rode a horse from Bilbul
to the Griffith Presbytery,
to prepare for his wedding;
what a happy man was he.

"The horse it was a bolter,
the horse it would not stop,
it galloped past the presbytery–
Bilbul was where the horse made a stop.
'The horse, she run too fast,
The horse, she do not stop,
I think I ride my bike next time,
Instead of clippity clop.'

"My name, it is Paul Guerra,
I come to Griffith on the train
to ride a horse like that Phar Lap
me never do again.'

"The Maitland boy wonder,
Les Darcy was his name,
because of misunderstanding,
he was to die in shame.
Les has now been resurrected
for the hero that he is,
One, two, three and four
were the funerals in his honour.

"Now that the truth is known,
there can be no dishonour,
Paul Guerra was a wonder
from Griffith, so it seems.
Because of misunderstanding,
they shattered all his dreams,
for good men who did nothing,
he was to die in shame.

"For good men who could have helped
put Caterina on that train,
to be with her beloved,
help him get well again.
Paul Lorenzo Guerra, he did marry
a lovely girl, my word,
three years of heaven on this earth
was all they could afford.

"For they then suffered tragedy,
they then suffered pain,
the Creator in His wisdom
has made it right again,
for they are now together
in that great place in the sky,
where even all the angels
happily did cry."

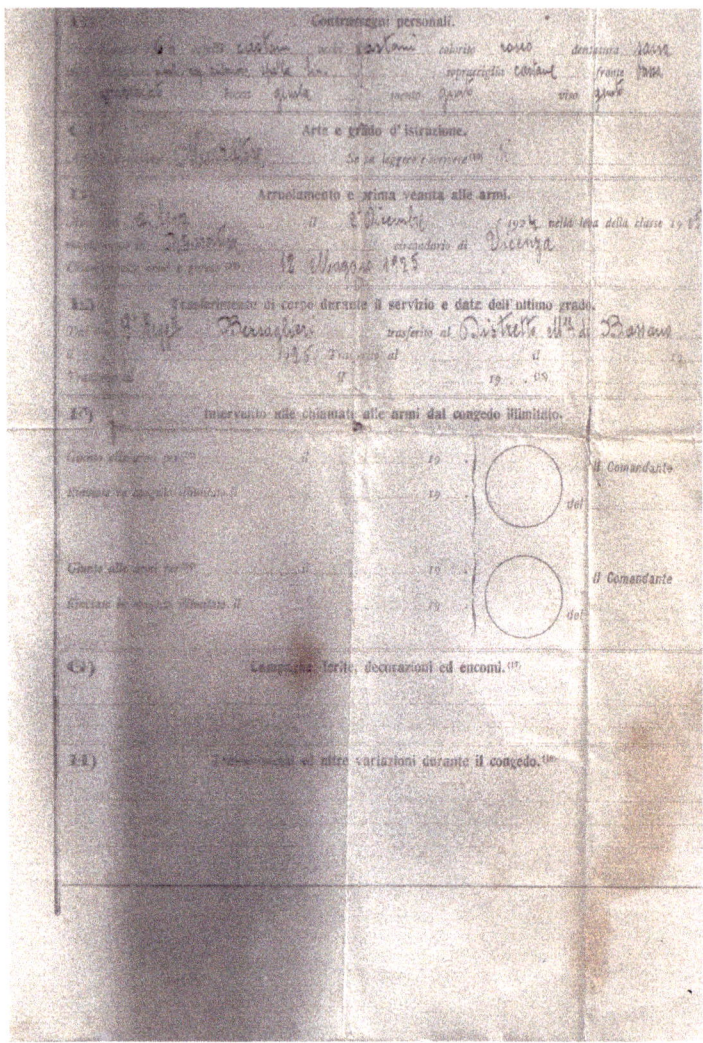

My father's certificate for his conscription into the regiment Bensaglieri in 1926

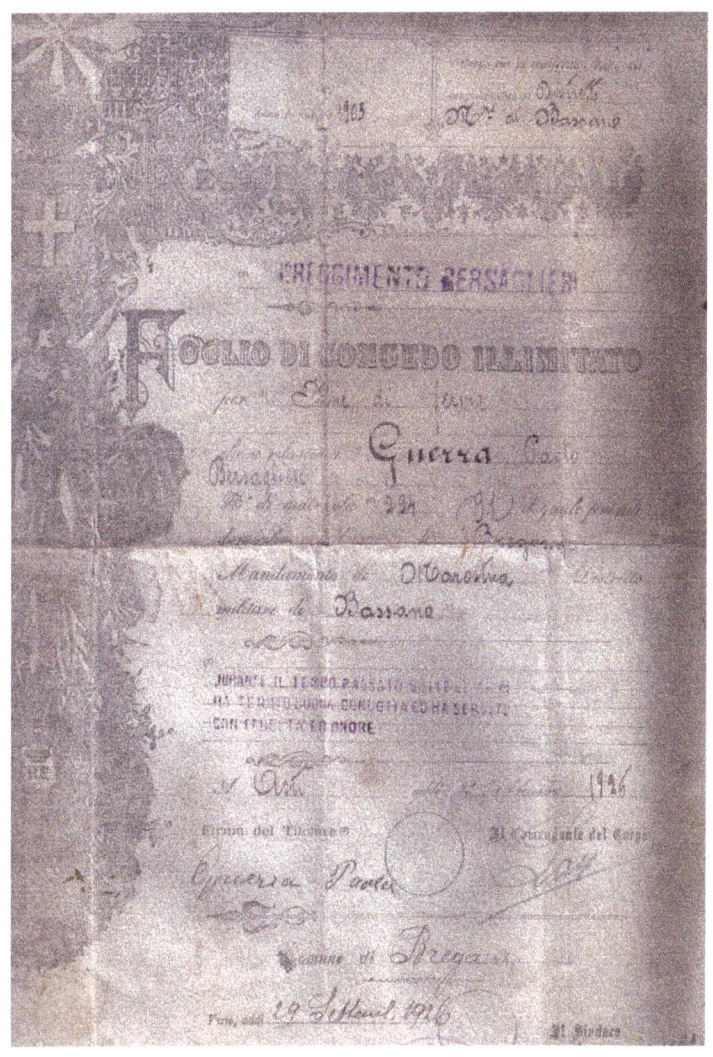

Mussolini declares war on Italians

At the time, Mussolini had not made his mind whether to plunge Italy into a war or stay neutral, whether he was to side with the Allies or with Hitler. Given that Italy had fought alongside the Allies in the World War One and the fact that many Italians were living in Australia and America, it was thought Mussolini, like General Franco from Spain, would stay neutral and keep Italy out of the war, or fight with the Allies as in World War One. It was not to be. His enormous ego and lust for power plunged Italy into a war they did not want. By Mussolini's foolhardiness, he declared war on all Italians living in Australia.

Italians in Australia went from being liked before the war to being violently disliked, and racism really took off from there against the Italians and against my family. The dictator's lust for power still creates divisions between Australian and Italian communities within Griffith and District. His attempts to convince the Italian people that he would get rid of the Mafia, bring irrigation to the lower region of Italy, and bring them prosperity if they were to go to war, amounted to nothing. Mussolini's lies and the racism that followed destroyed our family and I'm sure hundreds of other families within Australia. However, I cannot recall any family suffering the horror that my mother and grandmother went through. Some Italo/Aussies tried to convince me that Mussolini did good for his country by wiping out the Mafia. I would think that if any of his black-shirt fascists were around today they would know differently. The Mafia are very much alive and doing well, if we are to believe what we read in the newspapers.

Mussolini pitted Italian against Italian in Italy. The ones who hated Mussolini were called partisans. He was eventually caught by the partigiani (partisans), to be shot and hanged upside down at a piazza of Milan.

Giovanni and Natale Agostino taken out of the mental asylums

My efforts to get my uncles out of the asylums were not easy.

I had appealed to the Member for Murrumbidgee, Adrian Cruickshank, for assistance throughout the months of 1988. The MLA did his best, leading up to a refusal on 24 June1988 on the grounds that my uncle's behaviour might prove offensive to other residents.

However, constant visits to Bloomfield Hospital and speaking with authorities and also with one of my uncle's guardians, Sister Mary Trainor, my perseverance paid off. Whilst the Sister pleaded with me to keep him there, fearing he would not last long in the outside world, it was explained to her we too wanted to see him on a regular basis. It happened on 10 September 1988. Arrangements were made to have Natale transferred from Bloomfield Hospital, Orange, to Narrandera Nursing Home. I obtained the services of a cousin who went to Orange and picked up his uncle on my behalf. I had recently come back from Cooranbong, having picked up Giovanni Agostino and taken him to Narrandera Nursing Home.

Natale Agostino passed away on 11 May 2005 at Griffith Base Hospital at about 8.00pm in unusual circumstances. He was 94 years and 4 months old. He had a minor stroke at the Amity Nursing Home. It was my decision to have him taken to the Base Hospital in Griffith, where he remained for approximately three days.

On the first day, he was not well at all. On the morning I went to see him, the second day of his stay in hospital, he had improved enough for the Sister to say, 'At his current rate of improvement, he should be able to go home tomorrow.' However, the following morning he was not well. His chest seemed to be rumbling. I asked the nurse what was wrong with my uncle. The nurse explained that Natale had picked up pneumonia overnight. I noted all the windows were open; maybe that was the cause. I do recall on the first day of his visit, a Sister saying something to me. I do recall refusing, and she went on to say, 'We can go over your head.' I wasn't sure what she meant.

However, the paranoia was to come back at about

7.00pm that night. Two relatives and I were with Natale when the Sister said he had to be moved to another room. I asked why, and the Sister replied, 'We are going to give him a needle to try and clear the mucous or phlegm from his lungs.' We were not allowed in the room whilst this was going on. About this time, Father Beltrame came to the hospital. He took one look at Natale Agostino and said I should not leave Natale's side. A cousin said she would contact his two sisters and they arrived in time to watch their brother pass away.

It is not for me to say if euthanasia is alive and well in our hospitals, but the thought does cross my mind sometimes. My dear Uncle Natale was dead, the last of the tragic four human beings was buried together with his beloved mother and the last sad chapter of their lives was put to rest.

Natale was born on the 1 January 1911, New Year's Day, and was named Natale (Christmas). Natale had two brothers and five sisters, losing one of his brothers at the age of two. Natale immigrated to Australia in 1928. He was paged along with his family, by his elder brother, Giovanni, who came to Australia four years earlier. His father employed Natale as a farm worker on the farm of Block 737, Yenda. However, Australia was in the grip of a great depression and his father, finding it hard to support a large family, sometimes took his frustration out on his son.

Natale was a good man and a placid man. Sadly, through the efforts of the local parish priest, he had his first admission to Kenmore Psychiatric Hospital, Goulburn, in 1935. Natale Agostino was diagnosed as suffering from chronic schizophrenia, something that today, with proper drugs, counselling and understanding, people can still lead normal lives.

It is said that Natale, along with his family, would worship at the Sacred Heart Church, Griffith, on a Sunday. Natale had the habit of looking at other people's mass books during the church service. Complaints from several parishioners led Father O'Dea, the parish priest at the time, to organize for Natale to be put away. He was later transferred to Bloomfield Mental Hospital in 1942, possibly due to wartime evacuations at Goulburn.

Natale Agostino was to spend 53 years in different psychiatric hospitals. On about 9 September 1988, I finally arranged for him to be taken out of Bloomfield Hospital and go to Narrandera. I remember quite well Sister Mary Trainor asking me to please leave him at Orange Hospital, where, as his carer, she would take Natale on outings, bus trips and to the movies. Sister feared Natale would not last too long in a different environment. However, we explained that we too wanted to see him on a regular basis and that he would go in to a nursing home. For quite a few years, the Sister would send Natale cards and letters.

It was the same at Amity Nursing Home, Griffith, where he would make little dolls with the nursing care ladies. He seemed to like his move to Griffith, where he received many visits and enjoyed his outings with his sister, Carmela, or me.

The good priest would quite often call into the Amity Nursing Home and visit Natale and he would say, 'Come va?' (How are you going?).

Bene Natale would always say, even on his bad days, 'Bene,' (Good).

Natale loved to read number plates on our cars and other vehicles. The staff at Amity Nursing Home would tell me Natale would read the house down, especially in the corridors, and would also carry the *La Fiama* newspaper under his arm frequently. Although he was elderly, like his mother he would walk very quickly. He didn't mind a spaghetti and a glass of wine.

Natale Agostino's life was a tragic one. Like his mother, he touched the hearts of most people he came in contact with, from the nun at Bloomfield Hospital to the staff at the nursing home in Narrandera and the Amity nursing home, Griffith. Natale could speak English, obviously picked up at Kenmore Mental Hospital, where he was first admitted. It was surprising for me to find Natale would put away his clothes neatly at meal times. He would always wipe his plate clean and then put away his utensils. He would talk softly to me in either English or Italian, asking me what his sisters were doing. I knew a long time ago my uncle had not lost his mind, but the drugs I remember he was on certainly made him appear to be so.

After the passing of my mother, I felt the only kin I had was Natale Agostino, probably because of his great resemblance to his mother (my grandmother). I had spent 25 years with her. Although Natale was elderly, he did a lot of things my grandmother would do.

My uncle, Giovanni Agostino, spent 40 years at Morisset and the Cooranbong Hospital for the Criminally Insane. It is unclear how long he spent at either place. His guardian, a Mr Manfred Kempter, was a kind man, explaining there was nothing wrong with my uncle. He helped greatly in getting my uncle out of the sanatorium. He also assisted in getting Uncle Natale out of Bloomfield Hospital at Orange.

Getting my Uncle Giovanni out was not hard, but finding him a place to stay was. When we asked several nursing homes in Griffith, doors were closed. They told us Giovanni Agostino chopped his wife up with an axe and that he would be too dangerous to have around. This, of course, was untrue. A place was found at Narrandera Nursing Home. Giovanni Agostino seemed to enjoy his stay at Narrandera. Almost every weekend, my family and mother would visit him. Giovanni would sing to, and cradle, our son, Paul. His brother, Natale, would follow Giovanni everywhere. The nursing staff at Narrandera fondly called Giovanni the policeman because of his habit of standing erect at the corner of his dormitory. Giovanni and Natale Agostino were to be together for five years before Giovanni died at the age of 88. Natale was then taken to Griffith Nursing Home, now known as Amity.

South American sting

There was a time when my wife was not well and remained in the care of friends and relatives. At that stage, I had a six-month-old baby daughter to be cared for, named Mary Anne.

I had recently befriended a South American couple I had met in Sydney. I met the male singer in Circular Quay wharf playing guitar. I was impressed with his music and told him I could make him a star in Griffith as he had a beautiful voice.

At the time I was having a big problem with my wife who was suffering from a disorder. It was agreed he would sing while his wife looked after our baby. I paid the lady $600 per week whilst the singer played and sang around the clubs and hotels at night time and was provided a job during the day. He and his wife were also given a rent-free home and were well looked after caring for our baby.

Things went well for a while until the singer asked me for a loan to pay the rent owing on a home they were renting in Sydney. I thought about it for a while. He almost had me convinced. However, I refused, reminding him he was making plenty of money in Griffith.

The next incident happened when the singer's wife said she threw all the groceries and tinned food in the rubbish. It was quite a sizeable amount — worth about $300. She said she did it as the tinned foods were over two weeks out-of-date. I knew she was lying as I had purchased the groceries a week before they arrived. I became suspicious. That night I tried to prise open the boot of their car. I was unsuccessful. I shook the boot from side to side. It made rattling sounds. I was sure the groceries were in there. However, I could not make an accusation, so I left it at that.

About two weeks later, I received a call from my bank manager advising a woman had been cashing large amounts of money from my account. I recalled that when I put them in my employ, I left six signed cheques with the lady to buy groceries for them and our little daughter. At that stage I trusted them — I had the wellbeing of my daughter to think about, and also a very sick mother and wife — I did not have much choice. Upon receiving a call from the bank, I arrived at the Colonial Bank and caught her red-handed. The bank staff kept her there until I arrived. When I questioned her, she said she was sorry. The money was taken to provide for her children's birthday; it must have been quite a birthday party.

I was in a dilemma with a six-month-old baby to be looked after, my wife unwell, my mother diagnosed with terminal cancer, a large transport business to look after and forever collecting monies to keep the business afloat.

At that stage, I was not thinking too well myself. I should have made a citizen's arrest, but did not think of it at the time. I told the lady that I was deeply hurt and shattered and they would be advised what was going to happen next.

I did not have time to do that because the next incident was a very bad one. My mother, who liked to sleep on the couch in her lounge room, overheard the South American couple planning to take baby Mary Anne to Sydney with them that night. The singer had taken a liking to baby Mary Anne, telling me quite often that they could not have any more children. Later that evening, my mother phoned to tell me what they had planned to do. She spoke in a whisper — the cancer had been doing its work.

Hearing what my mother said, I went over to her house and confronted them. They had already packed their belongings as well as baby Mary Anne's cot, which was in the back seat. The man admitted they were taking Mary Anne to Sydney. He advised me that it was their right as they were now Mary Anne's carers. I immediately took our child away from them and took her home next door to my place and looked after her myself.

Next day, I phoned my wife and explained what had happened. It was an emergency. My wife came home immediately to take care of Mary Anne. Our baby's well-being was our first priority. The rest of the family were overjoyed.

The next day I went back to 23 Hudson Street and advised the South Americans they had to go. They advanced towards me; the big woman came at me with her hands held high as if she was going to choke me. At that moment, two homecare ladies looking after my mother made a timely arrival. That broke the deadlock. When the nurses left, I told the South Americans to leave the house immediately. The husband replied, 'We will leave in two days.' He went on to say, 'We have friends we want to say goodbye to. Also, I have to resign from my employment.' I foolishly agreed.

In the two days it took them to leave, they ransacked my mother's bedroom while I was out collecting freight money. There was a tin trunk in my mother's bedroom. My mother had been taken to my house next door for safety reasons — also for her failing health — leaving the tin trunk unattended. It was a huge mistake. The tin trunk should have been brought to my place. Although the tin trunk had been locked, it stood little chance against thieves. In the trunk was a large, white towel full of pennies and half-pennies saved by my mother over many years. The pennies went back to 1911 and beyond. My mother told me I could spend the pennies once I retired from business.

I think had I asked mother for permission to use the coins to save the transport business, it might not have been a bad idea.

The hundreds of pennies mother had saved were worth thousands, maybe millions, of dollars. As it turned out, I was right. The South American couple, within the two days they were told to leave, had broken the lock on the tin trunk and taken the large towel filled with pennies and made their escape back to Sydney. This happened about early December 2002.

The South American couple did very well with the towel-load of pennies from my mother's tin trunk. Investigations have shown that they travelled back to South America many times, purchased a house at Carnes Hill near Liverpool and a business restaurant where he sang and played guitar. We found out they were living very well. I would need to check out all of the coin collections within Sydney and surrounding areas, and probably hire a private detective or go to the police, which would all cost money. I have so much faith in the book becoming a best seller. We will wait and see.

My mother becomes very sick

It was August 2003. My mother lived next door to us at the home she loved at 23 Hudson Street. It was about 1.00pm when my mother knocked on our door, saying she couldn't swallow. She said she thought it was the pills she had to take: 38 tablets a day, seven days a week. This comprised Salazopyrin, Naprosin, Codeine, Panadol, Panadeine Forte and others.

She stayed the night with us, saying she didn't need to go to hospital. I booked her into the doctor, but we had to wait two weeks before we could see him. When we did, the doctor commented, 'My gosh, your mother has yellow jaundice,' and booked mother into Griffith Base Hospital. She had her X-rays and it was thought she had gallstones. The doctor said he would send my mother to Orange to a specialist doctor who knew my mother. The next thing we knew my mother was in Wagga Base Hospital, the good doctor saying politics or whatever sent my mother to Wagga Base.

At that stage there was no alarm. The thinking was that there was a stone blocked in my mother's esophagus. The specialist doctors would put a hook through my mother's throat into her abdomen looking for the stone. The operating doctor told me it was a dangerous operation. I was with my mother the whole time of her ordeal. For two months I had been travelling from Griffith to Wagga every day whilst trying to run my business in Griffith, while operation after operation failed to find the gallstone.

It was a stressful time for me, easily the worst of my life. In business, I had put up with my semi-trailers being rolled over, insurance companies not paying, winning and losing business, pallets being stolen by some of my own unloaders and even some of my own customers, but nothing, nothing could prepare me for this. I have never known a horror like what I was witnessing. My mother was dying in front of my eyes.

Then it happened. The Chinese doctor told me the bad news: there was no gallstone. They had gone down deeper and found a tumour in her pancreas. I am told it is about the second worst place to have cancer. In her three operations, as they were going down the hook must have scratched the side of my mother's larynx because for a week or two she wasn't able to talk. When she did manage to talk, it was only a croak. The last time they operated on my mother, she didn't come out of the ether for seven hours. I remember walking close to the operating theatre many times. When my mother finally came out, she was in bad shape. The hospital staff told me it was best if I went home to Griffith and they would give me the news after their diagnosis was confirmed.

I rang the Wagga Base Hospital the following morning and asked to be put through to mother. I was put through and the voice at the other end seemed to be speaking in a strange tongue. It was sort of garbled and it was as if my mother had lost her mind and did not know what she was talking about. I broke down and sobbed on the phone. I was a mess, I really was. The transport business was not going well: a semi-trailer had just been rolled over with a truckload of export oranges bound for Hong Kong. I was continually chasing money to keep in front of my creditors, which was almost a daily occurrence.

An irate truck driver was demanding I pay him $569, because after turning the semi-trailer over the police had charged him with dangerous driving. The pallet problems I had just got worse. I found I was buying pallets on the black market, just to try and stay in front. I must have purchased hundreds; no, let me change that to thousands, to get away from the daily hire of the pallets that were stolen from me. I think in 2004 I was paying 7c to 8c for a pallet daily. It doesn't sound much, but multiply 2000 pallets a week by 8c a day, plus a fifty-cent levy a pallet. The levy alone takes $1000 on a 2000-pallet hire. The 8c a day charge for 2000 pallets over seven days comes to $1160. I was averaging paying $2000 a week to the pallet companies just to stay in business with pallets. One unloader in Melbourne kept 1700 pallets. He, in turn, sold 600 pallets alone to one agent. After twelve months of trying to get them back, I sought legal advice. We met in court in Melbourne. I had to take three of my staff and a truck driver with me as backup. In the ensuing court case, which took three weeks, he was found guilty. I had won the fight, but lost the battle, as he declared himself bankrupt. That win had cost me $42,000.

Another unloader in Sydney disappeared with 3000 pallets and another unloader couldn't account for 7000 pallets. To his credit, he paid back 4500 pallets over a period. Another unloader in Brisbane took me for $24,000 quite a few years ago. I caught a plane and convinced him he should give it back.

However, back to my mother. I had not heard from the doctors at Wagga as yet.

At about 11.00am, I asked to be put through to mother, fearing the worst. However, when the hospital staff put me through to her, her voice was much better. What had actually happened the day before was that my mother was sleeping and the lady next to her picked up mother's phone. She was an elderly lady and could not speak English very well. Mother told me she felt fine. I then spoke with the Chinese doctor who told me the news was not good. I drove back to Wagga, where it was explained that after three operations with the hook into her esophagus looking for gallstones, they had gone further and found dark spots in her pancreatic area, which were thought to be tumours.

I was bewildered. Not wanting to believe I could lose my mother, I asked the doctor what options we had. He said they could take out mother's gallstones and gall bladder, snip out a part of her spleen, and also remove a part of something else that I can't remember, take out something else, and sew the rest up. When I asked what that would do, the doctor replied, 'We can't guarantee anything, but it could put six to twelve months, or perhaps two years, on your mother's life.'

I was confused and frightened, not knowing what to say. I was visibly upset. For the first time in my life that I can recall, I did not know what to do.

My mother had always been there for me in the past and I had taken it for granted she would always be around. This tragedy had come at a bad time for me as my transport business was on the ropes, my semi-trailer had been rolled over; a truck driver had tried to throttle me and the police had arrested me for assault. All this happened on or around the two months of my mother's sickness.

The following day I made a booking with my mother's GP in Griffith. I told him about the option I was given. My doctor, with no hesitation, said, 'Don't do it, Mario, you will kill her, she will die on the operating table. She won't last more than a day, or perhaps two. She is too old for such a big operation; her body is worn out and she has been through too much.'

He went on to say that as soon as they removed all her gall bladder and gallstones, she would almost immediately get diabetes. I had heard of people with cancer of the pancreas getting diabetes then going blind and not living much longer.

He went on to say, 'Don't put her through all that cruelty, all that pain. Give her lots of love and quality time; take her home, Mario, and spend what time you have left with her.'

I did as the doctor said and took her home. That night, my mother started vomiting and dry retching. The cancer was doing its work. Some days, my mother would not be too bad; other days she would look terrible. It was pitiful to see my mother go from a healthy 10 st., then fall away to under 4 st. I was with my mother throughout, but it was taking its toll on me. The doctor arranged for the palliative care people to help, as well as mother's home care nurses. They were all great. A part of mother's social life was having the homecare nurses visit her three times a day. They would give mother her medicine, bathe her, clip her hair and do their best to spoil her. Mother would quite often ask me, 'When are the nurses coming?' I think the nurses liked my mother as well.

Mother had two homecare ladies visit her for about 15 years. I think the government has definitely got it right when it comes down to nurses looking after the elderly in their homes. My mother did not like nursing homes. To her, they were glorified mental asylums where people went to die or go mad. Probably the horror of seeing her husband, her father and her two brothers become incarcerated, caused her fear of nursing homes. Mother told me many times if I was to do something like put her into a nursing home, she would never speak to me again. Of course, I would never do that. She told me once, 'I'm a burden on you, aren't I, son?'

I reassured her she wasn't and said not to talk like that. My mother became most upset on hearing her two eldest sisters were in nursing homes, saying to me and my wife, 'First I lose my husband, my father, my two brothers and now my two sisters.' Mother wanted me to get them out and for them to live with her. I told my mother that it was impossible, but she should go and visit them as often as she wanted.

About a month after I had my mother taken back home to Griffith, I received a phone call from her Wagga doctor, Fitzpatrick, saying he wanted to see mother about another option. Upon arriving back in Wagga, Dr. Fitzpatrick told me he could put another stent in mother in her lower duct, which could make more bile. If she survived, the operation she could have six months or maybe twelve months more to live. My mother asked the Wagga doctor what was the matter with her because up to that stage I could not bring myself to tell her.

The doctor said in a loud voice, 'You have cancer.'

My mother replied, 'Oh, my God.'

Mum would always say that in her nice way when something surprised her. However, five minutes later my mother had forgotten what the doctor told her. You see, my mother had Alzheimer's disease. In a way it was a blessing, as mother did not know what was happening to her.

My mother told the doctor, 'No more operations, doctor, no more.' About this time, I received a phone call from a barrister in Sydney who was acting for me in my fight to keep the business. He asked where I was. I replied, 'In Wagga with my mother.'

He said, 'Put her in a motel, catch a plane and get yourself down to the court house.' It was somewhere in Sydney; I don't remember precisely the place. The court case with a Sydney unloading company was on. It appeared I owed that company

$60,000 according to their administrators, whereupon I argued the unloading company owed me $27,000. Once again, it was over pallets. The company offered me 1000 pallets if I would give them all the unloading business into Sydney. The 1000 pallets were to be a permanent loan until we ceased to do business. My argument was that the 1000 pallets were mine in the first place. I had been paying rent on 1000 pallets for several years.

I was caught in the crossfire. I certainly was not going to put mother in a motel while I went to Sydney to try and save my business. My barrister was disappointed. He was almost certain we could win, but he understood my circumstances. Sometime before, about a month earlier, a truck driver had rolled one of my semi-trailers over barely 100 yards from the transport terminal with over 1000 boxes of export oranges bound for Hong Kong. The prime mover and the oranges were written off, the trailer was taken away to be repaired, whilst the driver went to hospital for observation.

I went to see him in hospital. He seemed alright. He told me he would be back at work on the Monday; the truck was rolled on the Friday. I told him I hadn't a prime mover for him. He said, 'That's okay, I don't mind working in the yard.' The driver came to see me on the Monday morning with his mother. He came to the reception wanting to know if I was going to pay a dangerous driving charge. It was about $569.

I replied, 'I can't do that.' I recall he let go with lots of profanities and racist names. He went on to invite me outside, saying, 'Let's get it on.' It was up to me to try and calm him. All this was said in front of his mother, three female secretaries and two male staff. I remember saying to him, 'Mate, can you cut out the language, there are women here,' but there was no stopping him. He grabbed me around the head. He was big, he was young, he was strong. He grabbed me around the ears, shaking me incessantly. I told him to let go, as he was hurting me. I was 66 years old and feeling every bit of it. The strong thirty-year-old was enjoying himself until I jabbed him with a hotshot. He gave a yelp and ran down the road screaming, 'You have stabbed me, Mario. I am going to tell the police and the R.T.A. on you. They will fix you.' I was to find out later his partner was at the time a policewoman. It was unclear what the R.T.A. was going to do.

A hotshot is a cattle prodder. It is used on animals to get their feet or bodies in position when they are on rail trucks or semi-trailers. It gives a short sharp jolt, which normally has the desired effect. I believe they are sold in some supermarkets and Dalgety and Elders. They are legal if used on animals.

However, my circumstance was unique. The big young man assaulted me in front of six witnesses — a truck had been rolled and the truck driver had not once said he was sorry for what had happened. My mother was not well and I was also concerned whether the insurance company was going to pay the $200,000 rollover.

I was tired and feeling very old. I was a married man with six children. The last thing I wanted was another bout of fisticuffs.

At 1.30am the following morning, I received a knock on

the door. To my surprise, it was four police officers: two male, two female. The first thing I remember from one of the four officers was, 'Mario Guerra you are under arrest, anything you say could be taken against you. You have the right to remain silent.'

'What for?' I asked.

The lady officer replied, 'For assaulting a man with an illegal weapon.' It was no use trying to tell the lady officer it was me who had been assaulted and the so-called weapon was not illegal and could be purchased in practically any hardware or supermarket store. It was about this time my sons were awoken by the commotion, and ventured from their grandmother's house next door to come to see what was happening.

I recall the police lady saying, 'Oh, I will go over there and search for the hidden weapon.' Thank goodness that didn't happen, as my mother was terminally ill. However, at that point in time it was thought mother had a gallstone problem. I assisted the police in all their enquiries and told them the cattle prodder was at my office in the cupboard behind the table where I usually worked. The police said I would have to go with them and they put me in the lockup wagon (or the bundy wagon, as it is sometimes called). After that, the police picked up the hotshot cattle prodder and took me to the police station in the lockup truck. It looked as if I was going to be charged, as the lady officer appeared determined to make the charge of assault with an illegal weapon stick.

I asked the police sergeant on duty if I could speak to my

solicitor and the request was granted. That, plus the fact the police sergeant on duty spoke to the arresting police woman in another room, saved my bacon, but not before several witnesses were contacted. By this time, it could have been about three. The police kept the hotshot in their possession until they were completely satisfied that I was not the assailant. However, it remains to be seen whether my wife and children will ever forget their father being arrested and taken away in a police wagon.

Shortly after this, I attended one of Griffith's largest funerals. It must have been about three weeks later. The lady police officer who had previously arrested me visited me again. This time, I was questioned about parking on a nature strip at a funeral. I probably was, along with dozens of other cars. It seems to be an occupational hazard at large Italian funerals. The charge was then changed to "backing into a dear little old lady at the Griffith Base Hospital" the same day.

By now, I was starting to think I was public enemy number one in the eyes of the lady police officer. I had heard of the Canadian Mounted Police always getting their man and it certainly looked as if the lady police officer was determined to get hers. By this time, my mother was in Griffith Base Hospital and my wife visited her about the same time as the incident. Everything seemed to be happening to my family at the same time. My wife, fearful of the police visits in front of our children, decided we should pay the $129 fine. At last, the lady police officer had got her man. To the relief of everyone, even me, I informed the police I was not a vindictive man and would not pursue the incidents through the courts, nor would I counter sue my assailant for assault.

At that time, I still had hopes of saving my mother and saving my business. With mother on my mind, it was getting harder to pay the bills. I shall explain to the reader why. Before the onslaught of the GST, fruit agents across Australia (mainly from Sydney, Melbourne, Newcastle and Brisbane) would pay the freight weekly and fortnightly. This enabled my business to stay in front by paying the subcontractor quickly. This all changed with the GST agents advising we would now have to collect money from the growers and packing sheds. Some sheds would pay freight 90 days and beyond; most would pay in 60 days. It got down to eight or 10 packing sheds that were subsidising the other 30. Going out daily to collect freight payments was taking its toll. I was offering discounts of three percent, five percent and beyond just to receive the freight payments quickly. I was slowly digging my own grave.

On 7 August, my mother was diagnosed with pancreatic cancer. For two months I had been going to Wagga from Griffith almost daily to visit mother. It was my staff who was collecting the freight. It was embarrassing, it was demeaning, but the wages had to be paid weekly, fuel had to be paid every 21 days, subcontractors, truck payments and tyres all needed to be paid monthly, and to top it off were the weekly unloading costs from Sydney, Melbourne and Brisbane.

It was with reluctance that I went under administration. It was thought we could offer 50c in the dollar but it wasn't to be. It appeared an unloading company had gathered enough proxies on votes to get rid of me. It seemed they wanted my head on a plate, they wanted blood.

It was thought a huge transport company, through the auspices of the Sydney unloading, would be coming to Griffith to take over all the freight. In hindsight, had I done what was originally intended I may still have been in business (which was paying the subcontractor's debt of about $340,000). I had $140,000 to play with and I had a good credit rating with the finance companies. I had the opportunity to not pay the truck and B-Double payment for three months. That could have brought another $180,000 into the business.

Sadly, if I had listened to a Factoring Finance Company and accepted their offer, things could have been different. Factoring means whatever invoices are sent to the company are paid within 24 hours. Their markup was 1 percent. They were prepared to wait 90 days for their money to be returned. However, I had already done a similar deal with my Commonwealth Bank Manager, mainly because I got on well with the manager who set up the deal. The two managers at the bank were good people and I trusted them.

However, at the last minute someone from head office pulled the pin. My accountant suddenly died from cancer and I was given 60 days to come up with $1,000,000 or the transport terminal and our house would be sold. With all that was happening around me and my state of mind, it was remarkable that I found a finance company to fund the money. However, it went right down to the line. With a week to go, we were given one week to vacate the house and hand in the key. Yes, I lost a wonderful business, but the bank also lost, with two fine men quitting. One almost immediately, I am almost certain. One quit out of respect for me, and maybe the other did too.

Shortly after, the original factoring company contacted me asking what I was doing. I told them the situation, and said I would call them. They still wanted to help me; they had seen the figures; but I had already put myself under administration. Also, an accountancy firm out of Wagga, specialising in transport was genuinely concerned and offered its assistance. The fees seemed extremely competitive, but it was too late.

There is a reason for everything. My mother's terminal illness put paid to that idea. I was to spend six months with mother at home whilst the administrator and accountant decided what was the best option to take with regard to the transport business and pallet agency.

After she arrived home from Wagga Base Hospital for the last time, Father Beltrame visited my mother every day, administering her Communion and praying for her. About two weeks before Christmas, there was a "Festa of the Madonna" being celebrated in Leeton, a city barely 60 kilometres from Griffith. My wife and our family took my mother to the front of the altar closest to the statue of the Madonna, whereupon my mother threw herself at the Madonna's feet. After the mass, there was a procession. My mother was so happy she shed tears, saying the carrying of the Madonna and the procession reminded her of her hometown Gioiosa Ionica in Calabria, Italy (where processions were a common occurrence). We ventured to Yenda where they were singing Christmas carols in the park. Yenda has an ideal venue for open-air concerts. However, my mother became extremely tired and we went home early. It was that night whilst I stayed near her bedside that mother asked, 'What's wrong with me, Mario?'

This time I had the courage to tell her, 'It's a tumour, mother. Only God can save us now.' I went on to say, 'We have won a lot of battles together mum. Let's pray.' Mother was very weak but still had the strength to pray. I had been under pressure from well-meaning relatives and friends to put mother into a nursing home. The thought had never crossed my mind. I am so glad I didn't, as there was a certain aura about being close to mother.

I must say the six months I spent with mother from August through to March 2003 were the worst six months of my life. It was extremely hard for my wife, coping with the children and seeing me in the state I was. I must have had several breakdowns, resulting in the palliative care sisters saying they were going to give me a two-week respite. I refused; I wanted to stay with my mother for the precious time there was left.

It became an effort for my mother to keep soft foods down. Junket, jelly and custard were all she could take in small doses. She would always bring it up or be dragged to the toilet. The nurses could not bathe her anymore. Even day bathing was futile.

Through all this, my mother never lost her mind. Whilst I would be dragging her to the toilet, she would quite often say, 'I couldn't hold it, son.' By now, the homecare ladies could not take my mother to the toilet (possibly because of Work Cover's policy).

My mother wanted to die at home. She would say things like, 'Have you picked the figs yet, Mario? Don't forget you have to cut them and dry them in the sun,' or 'When is Katie's birthday?' Then it was, 'When is Easter?' or 'Has my sister, Rose, come to visit me yet?' My mother was trying to hold onto life until these things happened.

I was trying everything I could to keep her alive. I would take her to places she loved to visit. One example was our old house in Yenda or the farms she had worked on. She liked to see the Yenda shops and would often ask where the old picture theatre was.

She wasn't interested now. I remember pushing her in her wheelchair around the backyard where she loved tending her different fruit trees, where she liked to water her lawns, but she only wanted to go back to her bed. It was about this time my mother said, 'Let me go, son, it's no use.'

I refused. I said, 'Don't give up, mum. You never did give up on me, don't do it now.' I resorted to looking for possible quack cures on the internet. There was one from Mexico where they gave nine enemas a fortnight with a citrus diet. Further investigation and reading the small print weren't encouraging. It was reported someone from Griffith in his forties ventured over with sad results. The cabbage diet was another thing some of my Griffith friends tried. They would make a broth out of the cabbage leaf and drink it, but they too died. Mother was waiting to go and I wouldn't let her.

My mother becomes very sick

What a terrible insidious disease it is, this curse of cancer. There is no understanding why God allows such a terrible plague to enter our bodies, but understand it must if we are to gain eternal salvation.

By now, my mother could not eat or drink. She was so weak she kept falling out of her bed. To drag her to the toilet was an effort for my wife and me.

My mother was so weak she seemed to be choking. I rang the ambulance after conferring with my doctor and mother was taken to hospital. My mother wanted to die at home. I wanted my mother to live even though she was suffering. I wanted to hold onto her.

Once in hospital, mother was put on a drip. She came back a little and was kept in hospital for a week. The doctor did say, 'This is it, Mario, your mother has not got long to go.' After about a week I was able to take her home. However, almost immediately my mother went down again, refusing to eat or drink, and unable to contain her calls of nature. A palliative care nursing sister said, 'It gets worse, Mario.' I recalled my grandfather on his deathbed at Griffith Base Hospital, white frothy mucus pouring out of his mouth. I have been told that even excreta comes out whilst dying. However, I received that report second-hand and cannot comment how authentic it is.

I called the ambulance again. Whilst wheeling mother out of the house to go into the ambulance, she said, 'Where am I going, Mario?'

I replied, 'We have to go to the hospital again, mother.'

'No,' mother cried, then, 'Oh, well.'

It was hell seeing mother the way she was in hospital, crying out to the nurses, asking could they help her. The nurses obviously had seen it all before. All they could do was try to make her comfortable. It was about this time the doctor said to me, 'Let her go, Mario, it's her time, let her die in her sleep.' All the time the palliative nurses were with mother; they administered her morphine, giving her stronger doses as the pain got worse.

It was time for the children to say their last goodbyes. Mother held their hands and gave them a squeeze. We have six children. The youngest, little Katie, was three years old. She was the one that had become especially close to her grandmother, possibly because she had all the same characteristics.

Katie has a striking resemblance to her grandmother in many ways. To this day, Katie asks for her grandmother. We noticed a tear in mother's eye as she kissed them for the last time.

Once cancer gets its hold, I am told that everything stops working inside. The body shuts down. My mother's face and body had become extremely yellow and both my mother's legs from under her knees were swollen and purple. My mother's feet had become more than double in size. Mother's cries of, 'Nurse, oh, please, nurse, help me,' were pitiful. She was now not able to recognise my wife nor me.

I succumbed to the doctor's pleas, 'Let her pass away peacefully, Mario, let her die in her sleep.'

Not fully understanding, I said, 'Yes, oh, yes.' I couldn't stand to see the pain my mother was in.

The hopelessness of everything that was happening: all the time my mother was in hospital I had been there most of the time, while my transport business was under administration. The leasers of the pallet and plastic bin agency were getting ready to defect and the transport produce business was under siege from other transport companies. There was not much I could do. I wanted to be with mum every minute, every second.

I was with my mother when she passed away. I had been so tired, fatigue had set in, being there and taking her to the toilet when nurses wouldn't. Praying always, praying with the parish priest, the good priest forever trying to cast the cancer out of her body.

The doctor and some of the nursing staff told me as mother became weaker her heart would slow down, she would be totally at rest, there would be no pain. I was there throughout. Whilst mother slept, I noticed a machine was put near her bed. When I asked what it was, I think I was told it was to monitor my mother's heartbeat. I nodded off to sleep and was woken sometime later by the sister who told me, 'Mario, it's time, your mother has not got long to go.'

I immediately phoned Father Beltrame and my wife, Jacqui. They arrived almost simultaneously and Father immediately got us to pray the Rosary. The good Father had seen it all before. We prayed until my mother's final heartbeat.

I accepted the doctor's story, 'She will pass away in her sleep, Mario. There will be no pain, she will be at rest. It is perfectly legal. At the most, your mother could live another day, perhaps two, in terrible pain.'

There was something angelic about my mother's death. She looked so much at peace; she looked almost young again. It was as if at last my mother was with her beloved husband, with her beloved son, with her beloved mother and father and brothers. It was about this time the good priest made his statement, 'Your mother suffered more than Jesus Christ. She was truly a saint.'

My mother passed away at 6.00am on Thursday, 5 March 2004. I was told to go home at about 1.00am with my wife, feeling almost a sense of relief that my mother was no longer suffering. I went back to the hospital at about 8.30am, and my mother was not there. I felt awful, and the nursing staff and sisters comforted me. Somehow, I couldn't get the machine out of my mind. What if they had not put my mother on that machine? However, whilst I accepted the doctor's story, it was the former parish priest who put the issue beyond doubt.

Upon my mother's passing, arrangements were made for my mother's burial. It was my mother's wish to be buried with her husband and her son in the same resting place. At the last moment, the council refused; three people buried in the same place was not allowed. The undertaker, the council caretaker and someone in the council told this to me.

Whilst I was devastated, on such short notice I decided to put mother with her mother. After all, mother had looked after her for the last 25 years she was alive. However, even upon her death, my mother could not find peace. On the

Sunday morning whilst I was attending to people paying their respects, it happened.

I received a phone call from a relative saying, 'Is it true you are going to put Aunty Cath with grandmother?'

'Yes,' I replied.

'Have you consulted with the aunties?' the relative demanded.

I was grieving, but angry enough to say I had no aunties. If I had, they could have done something about their sister, about their mother, about their brother. I was saddened by the phone call.

One pair of well-wishers suggested I should phone the Lord Mayor of Griffith, to ask if perhaps he could do something. The husband and wife spoke with the Lord Mayor on my behalf. The Mayor said to give him half an hour, and phoned back saying everything was alright and mother should be buried with her beloved husband and her beloved son. After all, my brother Raymond was only five-and-a-half-months when he passed away. He would only be ashes now. I am forever grateful to the Lord Mayor, The Honourable Michael Neville.

After the passing of my mother, I felt the only kin I had was Natale Agostino, probably because of his great resemblance to his mother (my grandmother). I had spent 25 years with her. Although Natale was elderly, he did a lot of things my grandmother would do.

A cure for cancer

'Will there ever be a cure for cancer?' I asked the doctor. He replied, 'I don't think it will happen in our time.' That was not very reassuring, even if it was the truth. However, if that is true, what hope is there for us still living? What hope is there for our children? My mother never smoked or drank alcohol in her lifetime and neither did her mother. Trying to find an answer to this perplexing question, I have come up with several theories:

The Bible says we should not eat the blood of strangled animals, the meat of animals with four hooves or fowl of the air.

In my youth, it was almost a ritual to kill the pig: fatten him up first, then watch the butcher go up through the pig's throat until the knife reached its heart. What a terrible way to die. One unfortunate pig next door to our place in Yenda was killed this way. As a youth, I watched in horror. It turned me off pork meat forever. Every part of that pig was eaten, from the top of his snout to the bottom of his trotters. What wasn't turned into salami was made into ham and bacon. The fat was all eaten and turned into fritters or cured with salt and other ingredients. That is something I like to remember: a great slab of fat or lard with a thin strip of bacon in the centre would feed a family throughout the winter months. Even the pig's blood was eaten. I remember mother and grandmother making a cake out of the pig's blood, using nuts, raisins and cinnamon. They were tough times and it helped people survive.

My theory: we should not eat blood or half-cooked meat with blood still visible.

In my youth, whilst spraying cabbages with Phosdrin, I made myself extremely sick. My face turned green and I was sick for days. Another instance I recall in the 1960s: salesmen would drive to the farmers' orchards selling their chemical wares packed inside their car or vans. I know of one person who died in that era, it is thought because of being exposed to chemicals. Another man became a successful salesman whilst selling chemicals on farms. He too became very ill for months. There were grave concerns for his health, but he was a tough man and survived.

Another lass working from a service station became extremely sick, it is thought from the fumes escaping from the chemicals at the back of a room within the service station.

Another man, the same age as myself succumbed to leukemia. He was a happy, fun-loving man who didn't seem to mind a social drink or the occasional cigarette; nothing unusual. I did notice chemicals inside a refrigerator with food where he worked. There was also a cut watermelon in there with the chemicals.

I know of two engineers who lost their lives in their forties. One was always smiling while he would happily weld inside the spray vat filled with dangerous fumes of Metasystox and other chemicals.

Another salesman who sold chemicals to the farmers died from cancer. Although it happened in Italy whilst on holiday, it is thought chemicals were the cause.

My theory: we have to live, breathe, eat and sleep with chemicals just to stay alive — it is in our meat, our milk, our vegetables — but we shouldn't play with dangerous chemicals (even household sprays, such as mosquito and fly spray) for our children's sake.

Another theory: stress is the cause of cancer. Coming from a poor country, my mother was able to defeat stress by her great belief in the Creator and that there was a reason for everything (for example, her husband being taken away from her). My mother lost one son, but she was young, she had courage and faith that her other son would amount to something. She needed to get him married and in a good job, and she had something to look forward to. As my mother became older and frailer, she picked up many sicknesses. She had to watch me struggle through my business, she knew I was in debt, she had to bail me out of jail twice; she paid all my road tax, overloading fines and whatever other fines had accumulated at the time. This was in the 1970s and mother paid over $3000 to release me.

She became stressed and worried many times. When

my mother had to retire from the hospital, it was about then that she picked up Crohn's Disease, an awful sickness which causes the patients to be on the toilet almost hourly. Throughout the night, mother seemed to be forever getting up to go to the toilet. This kept her in a weakened state. She would shake and tremble and feel very weak. I am not experienced in the causes of Crohn's Disease, except to know that it attacks the lining of the stomach.

It was explained our stomach is like a washboard coated in a furry substance, which traps the food and helps it to stay in our stomach for a short time. My mother had no such washboard and no furry lining. Her food would not be absorbed and would almost immediately go through her body. This disease disrupts people's social lives. My mother would refuse to go even to church because she may have to go to the toilet several times. My theory is stress causes Crohn's Disease, which is another nail in the coffin that eventually leads to cancer. My mother picked up many sicknesses after her retirement from her beloved work at Griffith Base Hospital.

I recall my mother had a stroke, leaving her with about 10 percent vision in one eye. She developed ulcers and she developed glaucoma, which was controlled. As long as I can remember, my mother had high blood pressure, which was also controlled by drugs. In her late thirties, my mother had a hysterectomy. She developed breast cancer in her late forties. About a year before my mother contracted pancreatic cancer, she fell off a chair cleaning the top of her refrigerator. She had a dislocated hip for about a week, but she said nothing to anyone. We found out about a week later when mother was complaining she couldn't walk and was in pain. The doctor said she had dislocated her hip when falling off the chair. The doctor said mother was lucky not to have gangrene set in. These were all very stressful situations, but nothing out of the ordinary that people don't handle in their everyday lives.

However, my mother's stress was a different stress this time, as she was not young and strong anymore. She now saw me struggle with a volatile transport business. Not once, but three times I came back from the brink of bankruptcy. She saw me finally settle down with a lass much younger than myself. She saw her son, because of a clash of cultures, leave his wife several times and go home to mother.

What causes these illnesses in the first place? It's the loss of family and friends, especially the loss of a loving husband who was taken away in such a brutal and unnecessary way at such an early stage in their marriage.

My theory also is that as we become old and frail, our immune system cannot handle the stress of watching our loved ones suffer. In fact, as we become old, we should not be allowed to have any stress at all. This should be made law. I am certain it would go a long way towards defeating cancer.

Building of a transport empire

My empire started in July 1969 with the purchase of a 30cwt, green *Chevrolet* truck in Yenda, to deliver kegs of beer to the hotel and club. After several months, I lost those contracts to a multinational railway from Wagga. It was my first lesson: there are no friends in business. The gentleman who sold me his town carrying business and his truck for $1500 could have known a bulk loading company was coming to Griffith and Yenda and decided it was the right time to sell. Of course, the bulk loading company could deliver the beer much cheaper than me. However, my affair with trucks started from there and I purchased another truck from a football coach doing similar work out of Griffith, delivering parcels to the shops. Whilst I liked my new venture, my co-worker liked farm work and did not like trucks much. Maybe he knew something I didn't. We went our separate ways, but remained good friends.

The business in Griffith quickly grew. I purchased

another two-tonne truck and it went from there. I purchased a 15-tonne *ACCO Diesel* truck and deliveries went to Melbourne. Everything went well, so I purchased a red *Dodge* semi-trailer with deliveries also going to Melbourne.

It was about this time, in 1971, a subsidiary of TNT Comet Overnite Transport approached me asking if I was interested in becoming their Comet Overnite agent, delivering their parcels with the promise of seven-day payments. I took the bait, with a part-time secretary doing the paperwork from home. I needed to look further as the business was growing fast, too fast. I employed the help of Griffith Typing and Secretarial Services, who had their office at the top end of Griffith, working from what was called the Crystal Arcade. It was a good arrangement. My depot would have been in the main street of Banna Avenue opposite the secretarial service. With no phone, no depot, and definitely no mobiles in those days, the ladies devised a way to get the messages to me. It was agreed I would drive past the Crystal Arcade every half hour and if there were messages one of the ladies would run out with a red cross painted on a white placard and a smile on her face. This would indicate there was a parcel to be picked up or a furniture job to be done.

Some of the shop owners from across Banna Avenue thought I was running a call girl service and, because both the ladies were attractive, wanted to know my price. I laughed, assuring them it wasn't anything like that and then told the ladies. They too had a chuckle. One of them said, 'Italians marry Italian girls, but love Australian women.'

Later, my deal with the secretarial services came to an

end and the several months I had enjoyed had to come to a close. Someone had alerted city council I was using the bay in Banna Avenue as a loading and unloading depot and I was told I was to find a depot or else.

The same thing happened at Yenda. My office was the Yenda Diggers' Club telephone, with the phone number 626855 painted on my truck, along with the words, Mario Guerra Town Carrier. This assistance from the club employees was appreciated, until I received a letter from the committee telling me it was time to move on and to take their phone number off my truck. Then, for a time I parked my truck in a yard close to the Yenda Hotel, which was formerly known as the Eric Pezzutto Garage.

I continued operations from a shed in Coolah Street, Griffith, and one of the ladies from the secretarial services offered to help. She worked almost full-time and her efforts were a great help. It was about 1971 and the business continued to expand. The lady found another secretary, saying I was going to be okay. She had accepted employment as the manager of the *Area News* in Griffith.

Shortly after, I sold the red *Dodge* semi-trailer and purchased a new *MAN Diesel* semi-trailer. I paid $1300 for the prime mover and $900 for the trailer monthly on time payment.

I accepted a contract from Copper City Transport to bring back semi-trailer loads of beer from Melbourne to Griffith daily. Shortly after this, I purchased another *MAN Diesel* semi-trailer to cope with the demand. All went well, the company was making money. By this time, I had two

Comet Overnite trucks to do the parcels, two semi-trailers, and another small truck to do the pickups from the Griffith Railway Station. The 15-tonne *ACCO Diesel* had recently rolled over a cliff at Dalby in Queensland.

Things were going well, with a contract to carry rice to Melbourne and Copper City and beer back to Griffith on a regular basis. The Comet Overnite parcels were growing bigger. For the freight I delivered from the railway, I had to wait 30 days to be paid. However, the rail freight on the parcels and goods would need to be paid before they left the railway station. Because of this, I opted to take the rail parcels and general goods off rail and put it all with Comet, wherein I would be paid weekly.

However, things took a turn for the worse when the second semi-trailer rollover occurred. Faced with the dilemma of having to bring back 18 tonnes of Copper City beer and 16 tonnes of Calamia beer on the same day, I opted to put the lot on the one semi-trailer, overloading it by some 16 tonnes. The result was that the truck driver could not take the turn at Jerilderie and the existing load of beer tipped over. This happened at night time. The following morning, I arrived with representatives from Copper City to find people with wheelbarrows taking away loads of beer to their homes. We chased them away, managing to salvage about half the load of beer.

Throughout my transport career of the 1970s, I had a history of semi-trailers rolling over, from a full load of bottles tipped over in front of the Punt Hotel at Darlington Point, to a load of carrots tipped over at the Hole in the

Wall in Picton. I had several others too, the classic being at Wallendbeen when two of the semi-trailers allegedly tailgating crashed into each other. This put the last of the two semi-trailers that I had out of the way. I was out of business. One of the truck drivers involved was also involved in an incident many months earlier. Upon sending him to Brisbane with a load of produce during a flood, his excuse was he couldn't get back because of the flood. However, I received no phone call or telegram to let me know if he and the truck were alright. After two weeks, reliable sources found he had been moonlighting on the Brisbane wharves. With no semi-trailers left and no staff except for a secretary and a man called Lex, it was time for me to stand up. I drove the Comet Overnite truck to Sydney daily with produce and back with TNT General. I did this on a daily basis, five days a week. Miraculously, no major incidents occurred, except when the four-tonne truck heavily overloaded with apricots blew several tyres. I had a passenger on that trip, a man called Irish, who said, 'Oh, well, if I'm going to die, I might as well die sleeping.'

We got as far as Binalong where the last blow-out occurred. With no more tyres, we stayed at a friendly policeman's residence whilst another small truck came from Griffith to rescue us. I saved enough to get a semi-trailer out of the repossession yards, then another, and the business took off again from there.

Kings Cross antics

It was in the mid-seventies, my Comet Overnite truck was highly loaded with car tyres, heading from Sydney to Griffith. It was Friday evening driving down George Street when I noticed a young man in a soldier's uniform I knew from Griffith. I stopped the truck, and greeting each other we decided we should have a few beers to celebrate his discharge from the army. After a few drinks, late in the evening, we decided we should see the sights of Kings Cross before leaving for Griffith. After tasting the amber ale at just about every hotel within the Cross and it being later in the night, about 10.00 or 11.00pm, we must have talked about everything including religion. We became prophets. With our arms around each other walking around Kings Cross, we preached to the people passing by:

'The end of the world is near; the end of the world is near.

Repent while ye can, for the small price of ten dollars, we can show you how to get to heaven.'

The passing throng seemed amused, laughed, and some said, 'Good entertainment', but no $10 was forthcoming. However, the crowd seemed to enjoy us in our inebriated state, under the influence of the amber ale, making fools of ourselves. We kept this up, walking the full length of the main street of Kings Cross and back again. It was decided that enough was enough. My friend would sleep it off in the cabin of the truck in the main street of Kings Cross whilst I would go to the El Alamein Fountain, at the top end of Kings Cross, find myself a bench in the park and sleep it off. I intended to do just that. Dozing off and almost asleep, lying on my back with no pillow on the bench, I felt what I thought were flies or ants crawling over my bare feet. I moved my feet quickly as if to make them go away. It did. However, something tickled the bottom part of my leg. I slapped it with my hand, still trying to fall asleep. Then ants or something moved up to the top part of my leg. This time I did not do anything. I was too tired, too sleepy and too sick. However, the next time, about a minute or two later, something tickled the private parts. I looked up and there he was; a little man probably in his forties or fifties looking at me with passion in his eyes. I screamed. I took off. I ran halfway down Bayswater Road. I must have done it in even time. I had never ever been confronted by a homosexual before. I reached the truck, loaded with tyres, saying, 'Gary, quick, let me in. There's a queer man following me. He wants to make love to me.'

I remember my friend with a cheeky look in his eyes, saying, 'Blow you, Guerra, you're on your own. I'm going back to sleep.'

Gee, whiz, I thought. *What can I do?*

My friend was drunk, I was drunk. 'I know. I know what I'll do,' I said to myself, 'I will climb up on the top of the truck and kick him off if he tries to climb up.'

Sure enough, there he was, myself on top of the truck, him down the bottom, still looking at me with that passion. I kept pointing my finger at him, saying, 'Go away, go away, I'll tell my mother on you. I'll tell the police, or I'll tell somebody.'

Actually, I remember the police did walk by, but they paid no attention. *I guess it happens all the time*, I thought. Anyway, I went from sleeping on a cold, hard bench, to the luxury of sleeping on tyres on top of a truck. The little, passionate man walked away and that was the end of it. We woke up late in the morning and made our way to Griffith. I loaded the truck next day, Sunday, with produce, back to the Sydney markets awaiting further adventure.

Caught with our pants down

One of the funniest things to happen in my lifetime was when I met a young constable at the Flemington markets in Sydney. After a few drinks at the market's hotel, we decided we would celebrate running into each other by visiting the Watsons Bay nudist beach. He was stationed in Griffith and was on leave for a few weeks and his knockabout ways had him in strife with his wife. He told me, 'What the heck, I'm half divorced, let's do it.'

I was single, so I guess I had a licence. Many a time in Griffith when I'd had too much of the amber ale, this constable would take me home. He could just as easily have locked me up if he wanted to after I had a night out on the town.

We went to Watsons Bay, where there was a steep cliff. To get down to the beach, we would have to go down a rope ladder. Well, that we did and there they were: beautiful women everywhere. Some were not so beautiful, dressed in all their glory with nothing on. I had never been to anything like this before. There were also men sunbathing on the rocks. As for the men, they were all quite fair. I don't think they intended to do much sunbathing. Most of the women were brown, from sunbathing too much, I guess.

Then my friend said, 'Let's get our dress off, *paisan*, people are starting to stare at us. They will probably think we are pervs.'

I couldn't and I wouldn't. My friend's pleadings fell on deaf ears.

'Oh, well, *paisan*,' he said. 'If you won't, then I won't.'

Just then a ferry loaded with school children (it must have been about 4.30pm) passed by. They were laughing and jeering at the nudists and probably at me and my friend as well. At that moment, I was just glad I had my togs on. Shortly after, the novelty wore off and we left. My friend took me to his relatives and we stayed there a while, then decided we should visit Kings Cross. After doing the main street a couple of times, we settled for the Beefsteak and Bourbon, a popular nightspot open twenty-four hours, just opposite the El Alamein Fountain. At the Beefsteak and Bourbon, we sang at the grand piano, laughed, danced and drank the night away. We noticed two very pretty girls at a table near us and we decided we would win them with my friend's charm and good looks, and my big mouth. It wasn't long before we broke into their confidence with my friend telling them he was Sydney's most important detective whilst I was Australia's biggest transport operator. We were invited to the ladies' flat where we continued drinking bourbon and beer. I must have passed out as I don't remember anything physical happening. Waking up in the late hours of the morning, my friend suggested we give them a $200 tip each.

Then my friend said, I'm a bit short of money, *paisan* (from the same town). Lend me two hundred and I'll fix you up later. However, I didn't have any money left either, so I offered the ladies a cheque. The girls didn't mind; after all, it was coming from Australia's biggest transport operator overseen by Sydney's most important detective. What could go wrong? About two weeks later I received a phone call from my friend. He was still in Sydney; I was now back in Griffith. My friend was in a "panic".

'Those two cheques you gave the girls; they bounced.' They have reported me to the boss. My wife knows about it too! Fix those cheques or I'm out of a job, and out of a marriage.'

Oh, me! Oh, my! Such is life, I thought. I fixed up the cheques and his marriage.'

My friend had paid what he owed.

Years later, I met my friend again, only this time he was a fair dinkum detective. He had been transferred to Sydney.

Razorback

The 1970s was an era of turbulence for the trucking and railway industries in Griffith. The growers were fed up with the railways and their unfair coordination tax and asked if I could do something. In the early 1970s the railways had a stranglehold on fresh produce freight coming out of

Griffith and Leeton. Nothing was allowed to go by semi-trailer road transport. Everything had to go by train within NSW. It was also an era when road tax was charged to the trucking industry. If the truckies could not pay the tax, they would go to jail.

Furthermore, the growers had to bring their produce into the railway yards by 10.00am to have the produce into the Sydney markets by 6.00am the next morning. With trucks they could leave at 5.00 or 6.00pm, go over the Victorian border, and still beat the train with no double handling.

I said I would do something. I set up depots just over the border in Victoria, where I had a lot of relatives and friends, so it wasn't too hard. I would send the subbies via the border. It meant the truckies would get into the Sydney markets sometimes later than the train; but the agents and the growers had had enough — we were succeeding as more and more subcontractors came on board to help with the struggle.

However, when a snap blockade was put across the nation, led by Ted "Greendog" Stevens in 1972, I incurred the wrath of the truckies blockading Razorback. We had several semi-trailers loaded with fresh fruit and vegetables ready for the Sydney markets. When word got out, Razorback Mountain was blocked with three of my semi-trailers and four subcontractors. We decided to make a run for it and try to get over the Blue Mountains. This we did, although we arrived into the markets later in the morning. Agents had been alerted there was no other produce in the Sydney markets because of the blockade. The agents scored a lottery and got top dollars for the growers, much to the joy of the farmers. I was now becoming a hero with the farmers of Griffith. Over $1,000,000 of fresh fruit and vegetables had been saved. The setting up of depots across the border in Victoria was also working, as inspectors were becoming tired of following the trucks across the border then to the Sydney markets. It was a loophole which assisted greatly in eventually getting rid of the unfair coordination tax, which said road transport wasn't allowed to compete against the railways unless they paid the railway freight barons for the lost work incurred.

After the success of getting several semi-trailers across the mountains into Sydney, an envious former subcontractor alerted the truckies of Razorback, whereupon dozens of semi-trailers descended upon Griffith. The Blue Mountains was also blockaded at Lithgow and most of the Griffith railway yards had been blocked. I was now faced with what was the right thing to do. Should I give up and wait for the blockade to end, which could take weeks, or take up the challenge and try to get the produce through again, thereby further cementing good relations with the growers? I decided on the latter. Because we were allowed to drive around Griffith with semi-trailers, we went out to the farms, loaded the produce and then at 2.00am we drove our trucks where the *Area News* stands today, opposite the railway property. The police station was about 40 yds. away. We obtained permission from the police, as at that stage no law had been broken. We drove those trucks ever so slowly onto railway property and onto the produce-loading bay, right under the noses of the sleeping truckies. When the truckies eventually did wake up, they were confronted with semi-trailers loaded with fresh fruit and vegetables being unloaded onto railway trucks. They had parked their trucks in Olympic Street. The police would not allow them to block Ulong Street as it was a main thoroughfare and also the police station was based there. The howls of protest and abuse, the blowing of horns and the heckling could be heard in Banna Avenue.

It became too much for one of the workers loading the rail trucks and he suffered a heart attack. He was taken to Griffith Base Hospital by ambulance for observation. Thankfully, after several days, he was discharged. The same thing was done the following night and, armed with a lump of wood, I stood guard over the forklifts whilst the trucks went out and picked up the produce. The only fallout the next morning was some brave truck driver had thrown a rock through the window of the transport terminal situated in Lasscock Road. At 11.00am, whilst we were loading fresh produce onto rail trucks, a utility loaded with several truck drivers and my nemesis (the former subcontractor) drove past us on railway property taking photos of me and others as we were loading produce onto railway trucks. One of them said, 'Got you, Mario,' as he took a snap of me. I thought the green-eyed monster was certainly working overtime on them.

That evening a truce was called and a representative for the truckies called to say we should have a meeting. The following morning, on railway property we talked. It was explained to the truckies that because of a personal vendetta between the former permanent subcontractor and me, the truckies of Razorback and West Wyalong had been misinformed. I said I certainly wasn't going to let $1,000,000 of fresh fruit and vegetables rot on Razorback Mountain. Had I been forewarned; the growers would not have picked the fresh produce. At the meeting, there were also growers. It was agreed there would be a cooling off period of several days whilst the truckies took their cause to arbitration. Then it happened: barely a day after the meeting, the Wran Government called everything off. The hated road tax was lifted and the unfair coordination tax was abolished. The victory had been won. The controversy that raged made headlines across the nation, including Griffith and Wagga newspapers and also WIN Television. Again, I was to become something of a hero to the Griffith growers, but not without a price. I predicted either my nemesis or I would go bankrupt as a result of the struggle. My competitor had to cut the freight price to gain the work; I was forced to match him. I understand he went first. His trucks were repossessed and kept in my yard for safekeeping. When road tax was abolished, it was a relief, as many truckies had gone to jail either in defiance of the tax or because they could not afford to pay. At the time, I owed the road tax authorities over $10,000 and had given serious thought to cutting the debt out in jail. At the time, I did not have the funds to pay. Some truckies had lost their lives on the bad roads, which road tax revenue was supposed to fix.

    The determination of the truckies led by Ted "Greendog"

Stevens and his blockade of Razorback Mountain spiralled across the nation, with blockades being put on in nearly every state. With the coordination tax (as mentioned earlier), I played my part and other truckies did likewise in the struggle to compete fairly with the NSW Railway Authority.

Much has been said and written about the nation's blockade and Razorback by other authors. However, the part that was played out in Griffith in first resisting and then assisting the blockade deserves mention for its role in helping get rid of the hated taxes.

It was now 1983, the New Farm Produce Act had been introduced, meaning growers had to pay a 2c levy on every carton of fruit and vegetables sent anywhere in Australia. A consignment note had also been introduced. It was rather long and, if not filled out properly, carried a $1000 fine. The howls of protest across the state by some 10,000 growers and packers could be heard in Parliament House. Ably led by grower representative Stan Hunt and Rod Sheriff from Windsor, I was called upon by growers in Griffith and agents in Sydney. It also meant transport companies such as mine would have had to check the consignment notes in case of mistakes, meaning a lot more fines for paperwork and time. Also, the growers' argument was the 2c. levy would soon become 3c., then 5c. and so on.

There were protest meetings held at the Sydney Flemington markets with Stan Hunt as the main speaker. I was invited to attend a meeting at Parliament House in Macquarie Street, Sydney. The then Shadow Minister, Wal Murray, was in attendance. We had another meeting in my office at the transport terminal in Griffith and yet another meeting at the Department of Water Resources, Banna Avenue, Griffith. All of the meetings were colourful, if not fiery. At the last meeting to that point, Tony Catanzariti and Adrian Cruickshank were in attendance. They were on opposite sides of the political fence. Mr Catanzariti represented the then State Minister for Agriculture, Jack Hallam. Mr Cruickshank was the Shadow Minister for the National Party. It was Saturday, 10 September. Mr Hallam was told by a delegation of growers they would not accept the 1983 Farm Produce Act. The meeting was at a stalemate. The minister Jack Hallam stood firm. However, this was only a preliminary compared to the main event that was about to unfold on August 26th 1983.

The meeting was held at the Yoogali Club in one of the larger sections of the auditorium, inside a boxing ring without the ropes.

The papers said 200 growers had turned up, but most thought about 650 people. I predicted 2000, but that was the promoter coming out. Among other things, I said the struggle was going to be bigger than the Thriller in Manila. At the meeting, there were reporters from Griffith *Area News* and representatives from the *Wagga Advertiser*. I had the meeting promoted like a boxing tournament, introducing Mr Hallam and the various government officials from Sydney, whilst in the other corner were the growers' representatives, Mr Rod Sheriff, Mr Stan Hunt, Chris and Vic from Windsor, and me. From the crowd were volatile growers having their say, as well as officers from the government. The debate went on until midnight, the vocal crowd almost to a man not wanting the new Farm Produce Act. Whilst the battle was mostly spearheaded in NSW, every grower in the nation would be affected. When the meeting finished, there was a feeling of confidence in the crowd.

Then on Wednesday, 28 September in the *Daily Advertiser*, Wagga, it was announced, "Mr Hallam Capitulates". It was a great victory for the growers of Griffith, NSW, and the nation. The headline in the Wagga paper read, "New Battle Lines Follow Grower Produce Victory".

The effort put in had become expensive — the time and trips away had dug into my resources. The grower representatives from other areas had been subsidised by the farmers. However, when my staff asked the grower packers for financial help, they were told, 'Mario has work, he should be grateful.'

• Mr. Mario Guerra . . . "The fight is not y over".

I was there when the rolling strikes of the 1980s occurred. I was there for the grower. The NSW Government Railways or their unions put on many strikes without warning. In the era, there were still growers who sent by rail, as the freight was cheaper. However, by assisting them, we were to eventually gain their freight as well.

It appeared ironic that whilst the freight business grew, my bank account didn't. After coordination tax was abolished, I was told I would receive opposition from other transport companies. I retained the work, but had to be careful and remain competitive at all times. It was proving difficult, as with the 200 small and large growers we had on our books, some subcontractors could do a sweetheart deal with a packer without the worry of paying daily rent on pallets or have to pay unloading costs.

Times were changing. The smaller growers with five acres or more were finding it difficult to stay in business. The bigger growers were demanding cheaper rates. Australia was in the grip of a recession. Loading back from Sydney to Griffith on our semi-trailers was competitive and scarce. It was 23 September 1986.

I opened a brick resale business alongside the transport terminal to counter a drop in return backloading. This became the third brick business in the town. From the start, the business took off. The business was called "Beautiful Bricks". I employed a lass from Sydney working in the brick industry to do a television ad. It proved to be a success, with builders and growers wanting to buy from the new sales lady.

However, the beautiful brick business became an Achilles heel with powerful growers telling me that because they gave me their freight business, I had to sell them bricks at a much cheaper rate, or else. There was a shortage of loading back with bricks, but to sell them we had to become more competitive than the other two brick companies in town. Competition was brisk and it was to continue this way until about 1991. However, with some unloaders not returning pallets sometimes for months whilst other kept the pallets, possibly selling or losing them, there was an extra burden on the transport business. Unloading costs of $5 a pallet were an extra problem because we had so many of the smaller growers going to different agents along with the larger packers. With them all having to catch the early morning markets, it was an extra overhead.

Match up your bricks — Mario Guerra shows his mother Mrs Caterina Guerra over his "beautiful bricks" yard, opened last week.

Opposition carriers did not have such concern in that era, with 6.00am being ample time to have fresh produce on the stand. Some agents would tell the grower packers that the produce did not arrive onto the stand until 6.20am or later. They said had the produce arrived earlier, they could have given the grower $2 extra a carton. Often, I had to pay the grower for losses allegedly suffered. I thought it was wrong. It was deceitful of the agent and the grower to take advantage, especially after the great struggles that had been fought on their behalf to give them a better service by road compared to rail.

With the bulk loading in the railway, grower and packers had to have their produce delivered to the railway by 10.00am. Double and triple handling often occurred this way, with the added concern of produce arriving at the markets damaged.

It was now the era of better roads and bigger semi-trailers. Since the coordination tax had been abolished, it meant fruit and vegetables travelling by road in NSW could leave later in the afternoon. This suited both the grower packing sheds and the carrier. It enabled the grower packer more time to pack more produce to sell at the markets, and helped them be more competitive with their interstate cousins. It appeared boom times were there for everyone. Something else was happening too. Grower packers now had virtually a 12-hour advantage on the same day to pick and pack their fresh produce, with trucks leaving at 8.00, 9.00 and even 10.00pm. A friend told me, 'You turned half of them growers into millionaires, Mario.'

Overtime became a problem, as more staff were needed. Phone bills skyrocketed. It became extremely hard to find subcontractor trucks when powerful grower packers would phone in with their orders very late in the afternoon. However, we managed. I became obsessed with giving the growers good service (even over-service) in an effort to hold onto the freight business.

Competition was fierce. I had very good staff, especially the secretarial and transport coordinators. Up to then, I had used four ladies to do both the clerical and transport freight coordination duties. This worked, as I could trust them. However, the smaller growers had just about disappeared from the business.

Several years later in 1991–1992, I got myself into difficulties for the second time with a staff of 14. The pallet problem was out of control and the *Bedford Isuzu* truck I had at the time seemed to be forever breaking down or tipping over.

I was forced to enter what was called a Part 10, which is part of the Bankruptcy Act that allows a person to carry on in business, providing they pay on time what is owed or part-owed to the creditors. I recall owing my creditors $500,000. I faced the angry creditors in the Wagga Chambers, explaining it was hard to carry on when some of our own subcontractors would poach work by bringing the freight rates down and others would not give us their trucks unless they always went to the same packing shed. Whilst no one wanted the responsibility of carrying the burden of the hire of pallets, it was left to my company to have the tedious job of tracking down the pallets.

At the meeting on this occasion, I was supported with all but four contractors wanting my company to carry on. It was interesting to note one of the four companies wanting to hang me was a large trucking company from the Blue Mountains. Right from the start, there seemed to be a problem with this company wanting to go directly to the customer, but even the customer was under threat of being taken over. The final cut came when gravel-like steel appeared in several bulk loads of fertiliser. The customer also lost work and incurred expenses. How the steel-like gravel was placed in the fertiliser is a mystery. Shortly after these incidents, I placed myself under administration. It took five years to pay my creditors the $500,000. I did this by paying $1000 a week. It took an extra 12 months to pay the administrator. All this, on top of the other expenses of running the business.

The fruit agents, appreciating what had been done during the great coordination tax struggle, responded by paying the freight weekly. From 1979 to the mid-1990s were turbulent years for the road transport industry and my business. Fighting for the right to defeat might did not come easily. From the start, I was impressed with the administrator.

'Piss the pallets off, Mario,' he said. 'Piss the truck off,' and 'Piss the bricks off.'

'They are what is bringing you undone,' advised the chartered accountant.

Whilst this was happening in Wagga, fighting for my very existence, I received word from Griffith, Wagga and other areas informing my major coordinator was busy drumming up support for himself in anticipation for my expected demise. Upon hearing this, I became extremely disappointed with that man. I had persevered with him after he lost his previous employment. Whilst he was not much good in the manual labour department, I gave him a chance inside the office on the phones, coordinating work between growers and carriers. After a shaky start, he became very good at his work. Being stabbed in the back, virtually in my own office, in my time, on my phones and my wages, galled me. Would it ever end, I wondered?

I approached him the next morning and let him know both verbally and physically that it was not the thing to do. He was fired and told not to come back. I was upset and I regretted the day I put men behind the phones in the office. The following morning, his parents went to my mother's house bearing gifts. They explained their son was immature for his age and was truly sorry for his actions. All went well, and he was re-employed. My mother taught me to always forgive, no matter what. It must have been hard on mother, as it was for me, but forgive we must if we want to live by Christian ideals. Forgetting is sometimes not so easy.

The business was now virtually controlled by big grower packers; they could dictate. In an effort to appease the sometimes-volatile growers, I was forced to appoint male coordinators. Whilst it was with some misgivings, it worked, as the sometimes colourful language of the growers could be returned in jest by the male coordinators. The ladies could not do this. Also, they would have to leave early to attend to their husbands and families. In being fair to them, the business had employed some magnificent freight coordinators; some have done as much to make the business grow as my endeavours over the 35 years. Organising trucks with growers and packing sheds were very skilful operations, considering we were virtually on call almost all hours of the day.

In emergencies, all clerical, secretarial and yard staff would be called into the office. We would work on those seven phones, sometimes up to 10.00pm in our efforts to get the load through. The years rolled on. The 1990s appeared to be good years for Guerra Transport Pty Ltd. Once again, the powerful transport companies (mostly out of Canberra and Melbourne) became a headache. Fruit agents owned some of the trucks; others owned several fruit shops. They would buy their produce from the packing sheds and ask to be topped up.

At all times it seemed to be a dog-eat-dog, cut-throat business. The only real advantage for us was the ability to take on all growers, no matter how small the load or how big. We almost never refused. That was our main weapon in keeping our grower packers loyal; that plus the fact we remained competitive. Our service appeared to be of a higher quality than our competitors too. However, some packing sheds still left us because of cheaper carriers. In the year 2000, to stop more packing sheds from leaving us for the cheaper carriers, I decided to show the competition I had teeth by purchasing a new *Road Commander*. It was a B-Double and was licensed to carry 32 tonnes.

My idea was to showcase the Griffith growers' produce with colourful sign writing. A Blinky Bill-like koala was painted picking and packing Griffith growers' citrus, with a large photo showing the different types of fruit and vegetables grown within the Griffith region. "Taste The Magic of Griffith", the sign boldly displayed. This was free advertising for the Griffith growers in the cities and markets, and I hoped growers and agents would appreciate it and further sustain my loyal base. It worked almost simultaneously. Another six colourful B-Doubles followed as well as another semi-trailer.

Once again, I entered (for the third time) the world of big trucks, this time bigger and better than ever. My friends warned me, 'Are you mad, Guerra? Haven't you learnt your lesson?'

Indeed, I hadn't.

The first two B-Doubles went very well financially. This was because we would have two drivers operating the one truck on separate nights. The plan was to give them three trips a week each in the one truck, giving them plenty of home life. Once a fortnight, they could have a weekend off. While it lasted, it was a good move. However, personality clashes and drivers wanting their own truck meant that after about 12 months the idea was abandoned. Each driver was given a truck. This also worked, only now we had to make sure the trucks were loaded both ways.

The trucks were colourful and were seen almost daily in the major cities of Sydney, Melbourne, Brisbane and Newcastle. The business grew to immense proportions. We still had enough work for the subcontract carriers and, for the first time, the growers and packing sheds seemed to remain loyal to us, so much so that I became known as the "Godfather of the Griffith Growers". Because of the better service we were able to provide, we enjoyed immense popularity.

The Griffith "Family" ties

I would say my first meeting with a member of the Griffith "Family" was not in friendship but an altercation. As an 18-year-old, I attended a dance at the Coronation Hall, Yoogali, a village about 10 kilometres from Griffith. It was a "progressive barn dance", quite the "thing" in those days of the 1950s where a man got to dance with almost every lady in the hall, if only for a short time. I found myself without a partner when a man moved in and I was out. I objected and pushed him away. We jostled each other. That's when I asked him outside. He did, followed by a lot of his southern friends. I remember whacking him first. His friends grabbed me as he came up with a knife. I noted all my friends from Yenda had left, except for one. He pleaded with the man not to stab me; things did not look good for me. That was until Al Grassby appeared. He spoke to the crowd and to the man with the knife. Al Grassby at the time was the president of the Continental Club in that era. "Flash

Al", he was aptly named, because of his mode of dress. He was an up-and-coming politician. He had become popular with the Australian and Italian communities at that stage.

Nevertheless, Al did save me from what could have been a very sticky situation. I was to speak with Al Grassby only on one other occasion. That was in the late 1980s when I met Flash Al and a barrister friend of his. That was at a victory party after a Jeff Fenech world title defence. Much had happened to Al Grassby 35 years later. It has been well documented how Al Grassby had become State Minister for Immigration. Also, with Lynn Gorton from Leeton, a city 60 kilometres south-west of Griffith, they did much for the Murrumbidgee Irrigation Area, known as the M.I.A.

I had always been on good terms with both Donald McKay and Bob Trimbole, having a small carrying business in 1972, delivering parcels with the staff into Main Street, Griffith, and other streets. Also, we delivered to surrounding towns of Yenda, Darlington Point, Coleambally and Hillston. Included in the customers were Donald McKay's furniture store; also, Bob Trimbole's Texas Tavern and his Texan butchery. I also delivered furniture for Donald McKay. Donald McKay was one of the first customers to give me a chance. Bob Trimbole came later. Whilst everything helped, I appreciated whatever came my way. I also had a Comet Overnite parcel agency, which took the taxi trucks to Coleambally daily. About 1974, I purchased a red *Dodge* petrol V8 semi-trailer. This was my second purchase of a large truck, the first being a grey *Acco Diesel*.

From the start my venture into heavy machinery was

fraught with problems. My first introduction into how fickle road transport could be could have been about 1974. The grey *Acco Diesel* was heading for the Brisbane markets, when late that evening, the driver phoned in saying the truck had rolled over a cliff at Dalby in Queensland. The driver said, 'Sorry about that,' and that was the last I heard of him. The truck and the load were not insured. It could have been about six months later the transport business was in trouble. I had debts close to $20,000, probably because I was not the world's greatest accountant. In one instance, a winery representative talked me into doing a load of furniture to Brisbane for $200, with a promise of a load back from Brisbane. It never eventuated. Good luck to him, bad luck for me.

I was becoming desperate. I had heard whispers about Bob Trimbole becoming a very successful businessman owning what was named The Texas Tavern. He appeared skilled in fixing poker machines, betting on horses and lending money. The banks were not interested in my problem and, armed with the knowledge that Bob and his family had been very good to my mother and grandmother, I approached Bob Trimbole, saying that I was prepared to do almost anything if he would lend or give me $20,000. Bob's reply was, 'Steady on. Hold your horses. Just keep your guard up and I'll get back to you.'

Several days later he did, saying that he would buy the red petrol *Dodge* and give me $13,000 and would that get me out of trouble. I said that it wouldn't, but it would go close. At that stage I did not care whether Bob Trimbole tickled the poker machines, or pulled up all the horses, so long as he could help me. Bob did, and it was done legally. I was grateful to Bob Trimbole. I believe several months later Bob's red *Dodge* went over a cliff loaded with wine or produce.

However, my next meeting with Bob Trimbole was not friendly at all. Bob walked into my office, which could barely fit four people. Bob was well dressed in a pin-striped suit, sweating profusely. He said, shouting, 'I'm doing this for my kids,' and put a gun at my head — it looked like a Beretta — and said, 'Where is he?'

I replied 'Who?'

He said, 'That John Jones, that's who. I gave him a parcel to deliver to Coleambally and he's kept it. Tell him when I see him, I will shoot him. I will shoot you too, Mario, if you have had anything to do with it.'

I am olive-skinned, but I was told I went a paler shade of white. My female secretary also went whiter than white, although I am not sure he pointed the gun at her at all. Looking back, I recall Bob Trimbole having several discussions with John Jones out the front of my office. Had Aussie Bob bothered to go through the right channels with my overnight parcel agency, instead of going directly to my employee, he would not have lost whatever it was, and I would have been paid my 50c. commission. When John Jones finally turned up, I told him Aussie Bob was after him with a gun. Mr Jones disappeared and I've not seen him since.

Another story I remember was about a grower who was his own agent at the Sydney markets. He said he would pay me every fortnight after he came back from the markets. However, having to go back to his place and arguing over a supposed late truck or a bag of produce that was damaged, I grew weary and told him everything had to be COD.

In that era of the 1970s, the Yoogali Club was the place to go. This particular Saturday evening, the little fruit agent man cornered me at the bar saying he should spit on me. A crown of southern gentlemen quickly gathered. He went on to say, 'Don't you know it's an honour for a Calabrese to owe you money?' It is only a dishonour if a man dies and does not repay his debt. I took quite a lot of abuse from the little man that night. I decided that discretion was the best way to go. I remembered only too well several years earlier a table service waiter had been stabbed very badly at the same club. However, his sons contacted me saying they would pay their father's freight COD in future.

Somewhere in the 1970s, my mother and I were invited to a Calabrese wedding. My mother was, of course, Calabrese, so I was half Calabrese.

The southern Calabrese in Griffith are very respectful when it comes to weddings, inviting almost all southerners to attend. However, for whatever reason at that wedding, I was given the cold shoulder. I did not know why at the time. I thought, *Was it because I had put the southern fruit agent on COD, or was it because I had declined several southern ladies their hand at an introduction. Was it because of my friendship with Donald McKay?* My mother also worked with Mrs McKay at Griffith Base Hospital. A clue to it all may have been while watching people dancing at the wedding, a pretty Calabrese girl smiled at me. I asked her if she'd like to dance and she replied, 'Yes'. Before this happened, her brother came up and said, 'You no dance with my sister. You no talk to her. You no look at her. You touch, I stab you.'

I was shaken. More was to follow.

'*Tu sae nu patso di marda*', a senior southern "elder" said to me (You are a piece of shit), yet another senior "Family" member approached me, saying, '*Mario te ta di amo* (We will stab you).

Looking back, I remember the pretty girl I wasn't allowed to dance with. It was her elder sister that I had been introduced to, that caused the problem. I told my mother that I did not want to go. However, her friends told me, 'Just pay a visit, if you don't like each other that will be the end of it.'

I went, and things went as I thought it would. There was just no magic. Southern Italians like to marry their eldest daughters first. I guess comparing every girl with my first love is not fair. Not to them. Not to me.

However, let us go back to the wedding where certain sections of the people at the wedding were hostile towards me. I told mother that we'd better leave. I did not want to alarm mother, but I think she understood. I was followed almost to the car. Perhaps my mother being with me kept them away. In Griffith, especially with the southern community, introductions by a messenger or an *ambassador* (ambassador), is very popular. Also, first cousins still marry each other quite often.

Getting back to the incident at the wedding, I told a big cousin about the experience. He became angry; he wasn't one to back away from anything. He bailed a couple of southerners up at the Leagues Club this particular night, advising them he would shoot them all if anything happened to me. He also made several phone calls to others.

In Griffith I know of several Italian men who were bashed for breaking up with their prospective brides. However, the incident, along with other things, had made me angry and worried. I sawDonald McKay advising him that I thought my person, even my life, was in danger. Don looked worried himself. I had never seen him look like he had. He told me he couldn't help much as he had his own problems, but I should contact John Doe (a fictitious name). I didn't, but Mr McKay must have contacted him as Mr Doe appeared at my workplace. I was on the phone. I noticed him at the desk. I wasn't quick enough to see him. He left shortly after.

Griffith at that point of time had become a turbulent town to live in. It was the mid-1970s, and there were whispers, innuendos about a big crop at Colleambally. People were scared. Then it happened. Donald McKay disappeared. If Italian people were scared before, now they were terrified. Italians were now being treated the same as at the outbreak of World War II. All the good work they had done, with hard work, trust and respect within a matter of 30 years, was gone. There was talk of Korean veterans marching on the wineries and houses of suspect southerners. I believe some wineries were shot at. I recall going to the Saturday night dances held at the local Leagues Club and being insulted by a Junior Vice-Manager. The young man could not beat an egg, but had something more powerful; his mouth. He tried to rally some of his members against me. I had to defend myself several times in front of the Leagues Club. Another time at the Leagues Club a well-known, first-grade football coach came up to me, saying, 'How's Al Grassby going, Mario?'

'I don't know, why don't you ask him?' I replied.

At the RSL Club, Griffith, a big man insulted me, saying, 'You killed Donald McKay.'

I dropped him with a short right-hand punch and that was the end of that.

The first I heard about the disappearance of the good man was when, on the morning sometime in July 1977, a local football coach delivering parcels told me and the staff, 'Looks like the Mafia got Donald McKay last night.'

I was shocked. All our staff were in disbelief. Australia's first assassination of a politician had happened here in Griffith. Almost immediately the papers had plenty to report. Not only in Griffith and Wagga, but the whole nation across Australia reported the great tragedy. Many books have been written about the disappearance of Donald McKay. There has been a Royal Commission about his death. I doubt whether Griffith will ever recover. Also, from what I read in the papers other cultures have tried to profit from the illegal substance. If it cannot be stopped, I'm afraid that Griffith's large Italian community will continue to be disliked. I remember a fresh-faced kid in the late 1990s asking if he could have a job, saying he just wanted to have a break from picking oranges. The lad was probably about 19 years of age at the time. He became popular with the secretarial staff, the workers and the fruit and vegetable growers. Everything was fine. The lad actually gained me more business with his good manners, handsome looks and Calabrese name. However, one day he left 10 pallets of produce behind and put 10 pallets, which had not been booked in, of his uncle Antonio, on the truck. A rigid semi-trailer can take 22 pallets only, which is about 22 tonnes. Anything over and the truck will be overloaded. Heavy fines then apply to the owner. I ordered the young man to take those 22 pallets of oranges off the truck and put the 10 pallets that were booked in, back on the truck. His reply was, 'I am not going to take my uncle's 20 bins off, I respect him too much; we are family.'

I remember telling him, 'If those bins don't come off, me and you are going to lock horns now.'

He said, 'Alright,' and that was it.

That young man was Pat Barbaro, on trial for allegedly importing, along with others, Australia's biggest drug haul. I prefer to think of him as the fresh-faced kid, sort of innocent, who wanted to obey and please his "Family".

Sometime in 2002–2003 the transport system was again in big trouble. My mother was dying from cancer, some big growers owed me large sums of freight money and the only way for me to receive quicker payments and to take care of mum was to pay between 5 and 10 percent to receive the freight money owed much quicker, otherwise I would have to wait 30 days — end of the month — which would blow out to 60 days, end of the month and beyond.

In my endeavours to pay wages, fuel and travelling to Wagga daily to visit mother, a city about 240 kilometres away, then returning home to Griffith and go collecting freight monies owing, sometimes taking me well into the night, I was slowly digging my own grave.

In the case of one "Family", it would not have mattered if I had offered 50 percent off their freight debt, they would always owe $52,000 to $55,000 dollars constantly. They would offer excuses, 'We have to pay for our fertilizers,' or 'We have to pay for our solicitors to keep some of our "Family" out of jail, or arrange bail.' *Probably also*, I thought, *to pay for their big weddings or big holidays*.

I was arrogantly told, 'We could get another carrier that would do the carrying, Mario.'

Thinking back, the staff of men and women told me they would work one month for nothing. The finance companies were prepared to wait three months for payments. If only they had paid the $55,000 they owed, it would have brought $165,000 a month back into the business.

Had I gone that way and not paid the five and 10 percent interest on what was owed to me on freight, it would have probably saved the business.

Earlier in the 1990s a fruit agent, an "honoured" member, got me for $11,500 dollars. After many letters and many pleadings, he just said, 'Sorry about that, Mario, I haven't got it.'

I knew the man had been renting a farm with about 20 acres of watermelons, so I drove out to the farm with the semi-trailer and asked a worker I knew if he would he put a load of watermelon cardboard cartons on the trailer for me.

'Too right, I will', he replied.

'The bastard owes me six weeks wages.'

I told the worker I would look after him once I had sold the cartons. I received little opposition from the "honoured" member.

Several years later when the incident was supposedly forgotten, I received a call from the same man asking would I do his carrying from him, saying he had a new stand in the markets and had heaps of money. I discussed this with a grower packer friend of mine, as to what he thought of it.

We both decided we would give him a go. However, a leopard can never change its spots, neither could he. Several months later I was left with $35,000 owing, and about $15,000, I was told, to my grower.

We didn't muck about: we kidnapped his foreman, then made him undo all the electrical wiring to the main rock melon grader, then told him to phone his boss, the "man of honour", and tell him what had happened, as we had moved the rock melon grader onto an adjoining farm.

The fruit agent was furious. He told us both by phone that he would have us locked up for kidnapping and stealing. The police did come. However, when they saw the rock melon grader safely tucked away on a neighbour's farm and the situation was explained to them, the police smiled, saying they were satisfied. The "man of honour" had been checked out by the police and they did know of him. They warned, 'Do not assault him.'

Before this incident had happened, I spotted the "man of honour" at a popular Italian restaurant. I approached him, saying, 'I want my money.'

I shook him up a bit, polished his head with my elbow, telling him the boys are waiting outside. He was shaking, saying he would have the money by 6.00am the following morning. 'Just come to my motel,' he said.

He gave me his *parola di honori*, (word of honour). I went to his motel at 6.00am the following morning. However, the "man of honour" had flown the coop.

I would now like to go back in time to the turbulent 1970s where I was to receive the first of three offers. It would have been shortly after I had stopped doing five trips a week to the Sydney markets with the smaller truck and had made enough money to get one of my semi-trailers out of the repossession yards. On this particular occasion, I was contracted to load a full 20-pallet load of onions for the markets. The owner of the onions noted my semi-trailer had bald tyres, and among other things, broken mud flaps, dents in the cabin and holes in the tarpaulin. I was on top of the trailer spreading the tarpaulin over the onions when I noted three men in suits looking over me. They looked rather nervous. I knew who they were. I later saw them speaking to the owner of the packing shed. The customer approached me, saying, 'I have noticed your semi-trailer is not in good condition. I know that you are doing it hard. Listen to me. I have an offer for you. I can make you more money than you have ever dreamed of. It will be like money falling out of the sky. You won't know what to do with it. Let me take you out to our farm and I'll tell you what you will have to do.'

All the while I was telling my brain, how do I get out of this?

I knew what he was getting at. The rumours in Griffith were very strong. I told the customer I would get back to him tomorrow. I went home and told my mother about the offer and asked her what I should do. My mother said, 'Come with me, son,' taking me to the room which looked like a mini altar. We both prayed the Rosary, asking God for guidance and mother told me what I was to tell the customer. The next two days after I had come back from the Sydney trip, I went and spoke with the customer, telling him, 'I am thankful for the great honour you are offering me. However, I will try to get out of this thing the honest way. If I am to go bankrupt, I will give it serious consideration.'

The man seemed to accept my decision and I still retained his transport business. I thanked God, I thanked my mother, and I also thanked myself for not making that trip to Coleambally.

Somewhere in the 1980s, I attended a funeral of a popular Calabrese figure. After the funeral, I was approached by a big man, not from Griffith, saying to me, 'Mario, why don't you invest'.

'What do I have to do?' I asked.

'Well, the more money you invest, the more money you get out. You put $100,000 in now, you get double your money. *Ma non parla*, and with a hand motion, he sliced across his neck. No, I did not *parla*. I also did not invest.

The last time I was made an offer was in the 1990s. A little man from a large packing shed, who had owed me large sums of freight money, said, 'Why don't you invest with us, Mario. Give me $25,000 and I will show you where the crop is. It has been cultivated and trained to grow under a pumpkin crop'. My refusal did not seem to upset him.

Those three men have since been sentenced and done time in jail. I believe crime does not pay. I also believe to mix with the "Families" does not pay.

Now that we had moved back to Griffith, a few things happened such as the colourful Griffith "Family" man holding onto $53,000 owed to me. The excuse the man used was, 'Oh, we knew you were going broke, so we paid the receiver the money as we did not want to pay it twice.' I asked how he knew that and he replied, 'We see the receiver every fortnight.' This man's boast was interesting. He had fabricated everything. It was a lie.

At the time, I was still confident of saving the transport business. At that point, though, I had not thought of approaching the receiver and was hopeful the $53,000 owed plus an offer from a recent lender could save me. The receiver was since found to be not keeping his books and records in an orderly manner. By his own admission, he asked to be struck off as a receiver by reports sent to me by the Australian Securities and Investments Commission. I knew the receiver to be a good man. He had helped me once before. However, once you are in with the guys, it is very hard to get out. It would be interesting to find out if the $53,000 actually went to the creditors or did it find its way back to the honourable "Family" man.

About May 2003, my mother had passed away and my two sons, Paul and Justin, and I were driving to the cemetery to visit her grave when suddenly from a "Give Way" sign a motorist sped right through. He collided with my car. He drove straight at me and smashed into the driver's door. I was hurt. My son Paul was also injured and we were both taken to hospital. Among other things, I suffered from shock and temporary amnesia, carrying bruised ribs, a bad neck injury and torn tendons in my shoulder. My transport business in chaos, a B Double semi-trailer recently rolling over, my mother passing away, unable to collect monies owing to myself, a finance company promising to assist me, except the $53,000 from the "Family", it was decided we live in Sydney to get away from Griffith and the misery that had occurred.

I forgot about the towel-load of pennies stolen from my mother's tin trunk and I forgot about the $53,000 owed from the colourful "Family". It took a long time to come out of the fog to finally regain my memory. When I did, we moved back to Griffith after spending over seven years in Hinchinbrook Green Valley. It was my intention to take steps to retrieve the stolen pennies and half-pennies.

As events turned out, about mid-2018, accompanied by my wife, I visited the "Family" man on his property. His refusal to pay made me more determined. I told him he could pay it back at $200 a week. The offer was refused. I countered by saying he could pay it back at $100 a week. Again, I was refused. Things got heated. I had my right cocked. It was on, with the man's son hovering close by on his forklift. My wife jumped on my back screaming, 'Let's get out of here.' It was a wise decision. We left before bloodshed occurred.

I will never give up bringing the South American criminals to justice. I am confident the sales of this book, which could easily be turned into a movie, will allow me to do that. I owe it to my wife and children who so much wanted to be part of the transport empire that had been built for them.

Wrong move

It was December 1999. I accepted the Loscam pallet company and became agent for the southwest area comprising Leeton, Narrandera, Hillston as far as Jerilderie, as well as Griffith. It was to be a great challenge. The rewards were to capture all the wineries' pallet accounts and also to make an assault on the fresh fruit and vegetable industry, intending to capture the business of fruit agents and growers across Australia. Ten years earlier, Loscam had tried to crack the lucrative pallet market in Griffith, offering the agency to my company. On that occasion, their request was declined.

It appeared the Loscam company did not make a great impact on Griffith during their first attempt to make inroads into the pallet industry. However, with the purchase of a B Double semi-trailer we needed for loading, I approached my appointment with much enthusiasm. Once again, I went overboard with a multi-national company, assured they would never sack me. I gave them over-service, as with the growers. Apart from taking their representative to almost all our produce customers, I took them to most of the wineries, as well as other towns including Hillston, Leeton, Yenda and Jerilderie. We left our depot open seven days a week, not only for our produce customers, but Loscam as well. We would service Loscam customers up to 10.00pm. Because of this, I am quite sure, winery after winery came on board with Loscam. Of the 11 or so wineries, only one winery would not come on board.

It wasn't long before Loscam wanted to move into the hire of plastic bins. I was told I would need a bigger yard, or they would find one themselves. It disappointed me to be told this, as Loscam at this stage had the rent of half the transport terminal and a good part of the main office. However, it was not all doom and gloom. With the conquest of most of the wineries, we were given two B-Double loads of pallets coming out of Brisbane every week. Loscam were also making inroads in the hiring of plastic bins. By now, I had purchased an old winery almost behind our transport terminal. I do recall being told by the NSW manager at the time to get myself five acres of land and they would pay $80,000 a year rent. It didn't happen, even with the purchase of the old winery giving me two acres. I thought even half that amount would have been nice.

With the purchase of the old winery, mainly for the storage of Loscam plastic bins, the assurance of work from De Bortoli Wines also came. The freight rates agreed upon were considered fair, with regular cartage into Melbourne weekly.

Payments were $45 per tonne into Melbourne, payable every fortnight. I looked forward to the future with hope. All went well for several months, until one of the controlling managers told me I had to meet $27 a tonne into Melbourne or lose the work to a large rival transport company that had come to Griffith. 'They're coming in with all guns blazing,' said the manager. I wasn't going to meet that price and told the manager so. I expected the "all guns blazing" transport to get all the work. Instead, it went to a big multi-national transport system. The local winery won, I lost, and that was that.

With the Loscam pallet company, a tremendous challenge was made to the Chep pallet industry that appeared to have a monopoly Australia-wide. Loscam received great support from Newcastle, Adelaide and Brisbane markets.

I assisted Loscam representatives by taking them to many growers, packers and fruit agents. It was a great challenge on the Chep pallet people. At Loscam, we were very excited. It appeared we had Chep wavering.

Although the growers were keen, as were the packers, the representatives were mostly told, 'If you could beat nothing, we will come on board.' They were told they would have to convince the fruit agents.

The rewards for my company at the time would have been almost unlimited loading back from Sydney, Brisbane or Melbourne, but it wasn't to be. It appeared Chep pulled a rabbit out of the hat, convincing the fruit agents they should stay put. It was open to conjecture as to what tactic was used and one theory was that some major fruit agents owed their pallet companies many thousands of pallets. It was perceived they would receive credits off the debt if they remained loyal. Another theory was the agents were told the Loscam softwood was not as strong as the Chep hardwood pallet and would not stand up to the constant battering of the forklifts. Another popular theory was a Chep pallet was worth a lot of money on the black market, whilst a Loscam pallet was worth nothing. Why change? It is thought the ones with the most opportunity to profit from a pallet were the supermarkets and fruit shops, when and if they were inclined.

It has been said small businesses, such as some transport companies, fruit agents and unloading companies within the markets, were the ones most susceptible to loss or theft of pallets and were the ones most likely to go out of business because of the inability to control loss of pallets. One such example: I was in the markets of Sydney with a representative for Loscam, trying to gain business. We spoke to a fruit agent about his business and he said, 'What for, why should I change? See that guy on the forklift? He has just picked up a pallet; I have just earned myself $5. We cannot do that with a Loscam pallet.'

It was an incredulous statement to make. Here was a man admitting to stealing a pallet. You steal when you were not stealing a pallet because the pallet companies were not going to lose on the daily hire. It was owed to somebody, who would have to pay the pallet company. It was like it was almost legal to steal a pallet. The law wasn't being broken, perhaps just bent. Some creditor had to pay forever and a day for that pallet. However, at the end of the day the war was lost. Chep won, Loscam lost. I do feel the biggest loser was me. I purchased many trucks in anticipation of the expected victory. I had travelled to many markets including Sydney, Newcastle, Brisbane and Adelaide, and attended many meetings. However, the pain was softened by Loscam's successful assault on the plastic bin industry.

In a short time, it grew to astronomical proportions to become arguably the biggest hirer of plastic bins within the nation. My company had plenty of loading back from the cities, building a large pool of bins and stockpiling them in our depot in Lassock Road and our new depot in Shaw Road behind the main depot. While it lasted, the work was good, even if the freight rates were cheap. We needed a quick turnaround as the trucks were needed daily to load produce. However, my faith in Loscam started to waver again when they announced they were appointing an agent in the township of Leeton. They sent a logistics man down to allay my concerns as my written contract definitely said, Agent for the South West Region, which covered Leeton and further afield. He assured me he would beat his drum for Mario Guerra all the way to head office and beat it he did. I had nothing but respect for that man. After all, I initially put Loscam on the map in Griffith. I was told because of the great contribution I had made it would not be out of order to put in for a rise, considering I had just lost all the Leeton work. I was told I had received 98 percent of what I had asked. However, my accountant at the time disagreed, saying we only received 32 percent. Obviously, one of the parties got it wrong. I put in for another rise, one of the main reasons being to quell the disenchantment the working staff had with Loscam. With one secretary being tied up almost full-time, several of the working staff also full-time, forklift gas and overtime, my staff was concerned about the viability of Loscam. They were more concerned about their jobs, and with one staff member making his feelings known publicly, it didn't help my cause much. I had given my all for Loscam. Almost three parts of the transport terminal had been taken by Loscam. Part of the depot was turned into a showroom.

I had purchased an old winery at the back of our property, almost two acres for Loscam. We also parked our semi-trailers there, but only with Loscam's permission. It was not uncommon to have up to 20,000 bins in the off-season in our depots for the honour of Loscam.

Initially, in my attempt to please both the grower and fruit agents, I built the terminal to look like Sydney markets. The large wingspan was about half the size of Newcastle markets, and as with Flemington markets there were placards of fruit agents and growers on display throughout the terminal. With Loscam, it was the same. It was my intention to give the Loscam customer the best of service, so an extra double forklift was ordered. If powerful wineries wanted pallets at 10.30pm, it was done. Also, Loscam was proudly displayed on our trucks with signs on placards placed throughout our terminal. I had tried to allow the Loscam customer and semi-trailers to have half the shed because most of the growers' produce was now loaded out on farms with our semi B-Doubles and our subcontractors. In my wisdom, it should have worked, but this was not always the case.

Blood was spilled for Loscam, bad blood, in my attempts to ask a worker to move a yard truck from the Loscam area and take it to the produce section. I was resisted; the worker wanted to unload the truck where it was. He continued unloading the truck in the Loscam section, so this time I demanded the truck was unloaded in the produce section. With what looked like a snarl, he showed me the rope from the truck. I became alarmed; I told him to leave the premises. I recall saying this several times. Instead, he stormed into the office, throwing $2 at me and saying he was going to make a phone call. I thought he also said he wanted more money to work here anyhow. I should have left it there. However, I too had lost my cool. After he made his phone call, he walked out of the office towards me. I said again, 'Leave the premises.'

He replied, 'Make me.'

He was a big, young man, about 29 years old, and it was not the first time we had locked horns. About a year earlier, I had employed this man to work in the challenging job of becoming a freight coordinator. He showed promise, but was not our cup of tea.

Twelve months earlier he had entered my office, stood in front of me, and demanded to be paid what he claimed was unpaid wages. I asked him to leave, but instead a scuffle occurred. After a little while, I connected a good punch with his chin and he went down. A few seconds later, he got up with a mobile in his hand, dialling the police. He also called his mother. He appeared to be limping. The police arrived and, upon hearing his story about an alleged assault, they looked at him, then me, and told him he was to leave the premises. They said an owner of a property had every right to ask a trespasser to leave, even if it meant getting physical, so long as the offender wasn't seriously hurt.

Many months later, I required an assistant freight coordinator. I went through an employment agency and the big young man's application was there as well. After studying it, along with the other applicants, I decided to give him another chance. My thinking was, he was an only son like me and we all make mistakes. The staff welcomed him, and once again everything went well for a while, then the mistakes started happening. An amount of $9000 and more had to be paid back to growers. Freight consigned to Melbourne finished in Brisbane and Sydney freight finished up in Melbourne. The other two coordinators were extremely experienced, having been coordinating for over 15 years, so I decided to give the big young man a smaller truck for picking up produce on farms and bringing it to the terminal.

Thinking back, it was a mistake for him to apply and a bigger mistake to employ him. Earlier, he had assaulted a truck driver. A secretary tried to stop him and it is said she too was hit, although she denies it ever happened.

Unfair Dismissal laws were at their best for the employee during that era of 2003. It took three letters and several warnings before someone could be dismissed. Most employees are worth their weight in gold, why would a boss want to dismiss them? It would have to be something very bad. It turned out to be exactly that. I said, 'Leave the premises for the last time.'

Looking over the top of me, he replied, 'Make me.'

I was wearing thongs and, very angry at him, I took a swing and missed by the proverbial mile. However, he didn't. It was a good punch and it put me down. It was the first time I had ever been knocked down in a street fight, but more was to follow. I got up, and enraged, I chased him throwing wild punches everywhere. I missed with everyone. The big man counter-punched me beautifully, he whacked me with another couple of good punches and I went down again. I got up, but got thrown down. This time the big man laid his boots into me, I was kicked over my face and all over my back; my ribs felt broken, as did my chest. Two terrified truckies, a scared yardman, two freight coordinators and a secretary watched it all. None of them would come out. I got up once more and went after him, hoping he would get tired from hitting and kicking me. He grabbed me once more and threw me to the ground. This time, I was able to grab him and take him with me. We both went down hard, our heads narrowly missing the corner of a Loscam wooden pallet.

The young man groaned as we went down. He got up quicker than I could and continued to kick me all over my face and body. To get away from the kicks, my only chance was to roll under a semi-trailer. I came out the other side and I remember leaping onto the semi-trailer then jumping off. I went towards him again. He said, 'You have had enough, Mario.'

As he walked away, he appeared to be limping.

I certainly did have enough. My time had come, I was a

mess. I thought my ribs had been broken and my face was starting to swell, a legacy of the kicks and punches I had taken. I felt like an old gunfighter facing a young gunslinger. I remembered the words a man called Southgate had said to me 40 years earlier, 'One day, Mario, some young man is going to give you the beating of your life.' I couldn't see it then, and told him so. His prophecy was chillingly right. At 66 years old, I may have beaten the big 29-year-old had I elected to box him and waited my chance. However, I had lost my temper. I was almost glad I lost. I had had enough.

I never gave up. I wasn't scared of him or anybody. I'm proud of that. It's a legacy of my days in Yenda when as a schoolboy I would run away from the racist thugs that infested Yenda then. I wanted so much not to be afraid of them, and several years later, I wasn't.

After the incident, I went home and attended to my wounds, vowing I would never fight again, no matter what. My 18-year-old, when finding out what had happened, was furious. He demanded to know why no one helped stop the slaughter.

'It doesn't work that way, son.'

I explained that in a street fight you are in it by yourself, even to the death. That night I received a phone call from my conqueror, asking me to forget about what happened and asking if he could have his job back. I recall saying, 'Not likely, but if you can do me the honour of one more time, I would consider it.'

'What?' he replied, 'and I suppose I have to stand there in front of you while you beat me up?'

'No, no,' I replied, 'I need to know who is the best one in a fair fight.'

'I will beat you again,' he replied and hung up.

Several days later, I received a summons to appear before a tribunal for an Unfair Dismissal charge, among other things. I was also mentioned as a registered pugilist. The barrister acting for me was baffled. 'What is a registered pugilist?' he asked. At my age, I wasn't quite sure what it was. Within NSW I do believe boxers are not allowed to fight after the age of 35. Also, the gentleman's claim for unfair dismissal could not stand up. We paid our legal fees and walked away forever. Sadly, several years later this young man lost his life in a tragic trucking accident.

Looking back, in hindsight, had I never taken on the Loscam pallet and plastic bin agency, I may still be in business today. Loscam certainly did not do me any favours. When it came to my time of needing their agency and rent for the property I had purchased in Shaw Road, mainly for Loscam storage of plastic bins and pallets, it was not to be. They stalled and stayed until they found somewhere else suitable. That's business I suppose. There are no friends in business, as I was to find out in the harshest of ways.

With my business well and truly under administration, I would have thought Loscam management could have shown a mark of respect on the day of my mother's funeral by closing for the day. After all, if it wasn't for the efforts of my fellow workers and me, Loscam may very well never have come to Griffith. It wasn't to be. It was business as usual, except for the determination of a secretary who insisted the terminal close down for at least the mass service. I don't think it put Loscam or the Area Manager in a good light.

Disgusted with Loscam's decision, I removed almost all the pallets and plastic bins from the main transport terminal in Lasscock Road and brought them to the Shaw Road property. Everything was under lock and chain. All of a sudden, Loscam was looking vulnerable. It was my intention to start legal proceedings for breach of contract. Loscam countered by threatening to sue me for loss of livelihood, which was, of course, impossible due to my situation.

The charade continued for almost two weeks until I received a phone call from a very upset administrator. 'What on earth are you doing? Whatever it is, DON'T. It's not worth going to jail for,' said the irate administrator.

'Why?' I wanted to know. 'They can't sue me and I can make a lot of money selling Loscam plastic bins,' I replied in jest. However, whilst it appeared nothing much worse could have happened to me, the legal team working for Loscam threatened to take action against the administrator and his company if I did not release the plastic bins and pallets.

I had a lot of respect for that man. I did not want him or his company to fall into disrepute on my account. Reluctantly, I released everything belonging to Loscam.

True love

It started in October 1987 at an Italo-Spanish dance held at the Yoogali Club, Griffith, where I met my newest lady love. Later, she became my wife. Urged on by her brother to ask her for a dance, I went for it. The pretty lass was much younger than me, but at the time I was known as Griffith's oldest teenager. I owned a flash Targa Top *Supra* and wore a white hat. All went well, except for the language barrier. She was from South America, and my Italian and her South American made talking difficult. She agreed to go with me on a date. We arranged to go to the Bagtown Inn for dinner. Thinking the South American custom was like the Southern Calabrese, I asked her brother and her mother if they would like to chaperone us. Their reply was, 'If you aren't old enough to go out by yourselves now, you never will be.'

We dined at the restaurant and after having too much to drink, I commenced telling my date what a wonderful person I was. We still talk about how I told my girlfriend if she played her cards right, I might marry her. My girlfriend looked at me, she listened, she seemed amazed at what she was hearing and she waited patiently until I was finished. I remember her saying in South American, 'I can't go with a man like you, you are too full of yourself, take me home.' My date was a disaster, I never received my expected goodnight kiss, and that was that.

We hardly saw each other for two years after that. She had been married and separated when we had gone out on our first date. I would see her from time to time packing oranges and carrots at packing sheds and her looks told me she was still interested. At that stage I wasn't sure. She had been married and had a child from the union. She was much younger than me; would she go back to her husband? I was in a dilemma; it was now or never for me. I was 50 years old and my yearning to take a wife and start a family was still very strong. I thought I had chances with several other younger available ladies in town, then again, I wasn't sure. They were career women. Would they give me a child and if they did, would I have to wait 10 years whilst they got their career on track? Would they wear the pants? Would I have to do as I was told? At my age, I had become fussy and insecure; I seemed more content walking my dog. However, I couldn't forget the South American girl with the pretty face and flashing eyes.

One day she came to the office and asked my secretary if she could see me.

'There's someone here who wants to see you,' the secretary said, with a teasing smile. She came into my office looking like a princess. She was wearing a pale pink outfit and she seemed content to sit in her chair, smile and look at me. Not many words were spoken.

It took off from there. I took her out quite regularly. I took her to the Copacabana at Wagga and we went on several trips to Sydney, as well as to some of the restaurants and clubs in Griffith. At first, I was nervous taking my newest young girlfriend out in Griffith, wondering how society would judge me, a man about town squiring a pretty lass much younger than himself.

The climax came for me when I took my girlfriend to the Regional Theatre in Griffith. There would be many high-profile people there. When I picked her up, she looked (as always) prettier than a pretty picture. However, this time she looked younger than her 23 years. She looked about 16. Jacqui, my girlfriend, had her hair done in plaits with one on each side of her shoulders. 'Ouch,' I said to myself. Jacqui asked if I liked her new hairstyle. Of course, I said I liked it, and I did.

I was just about to prove how much I did like it by taking my new girlfriend to the Regional Theatre. As we sat down in our chairs, we were in front of the Town Mayor and the local member for the National Party. We exchanged greetings and that was that. We genuinely liked each other, not her youth or my age were going to stop that, not even my friends ribbing me, saying things like, 'She will put you in the grave in six months' time Guerra,' or 'She will leave you for a younger man after she has all your money.'

Up to that point, it seemed all right with her mother and

brother. Her brother seemed to live by his wits. He gained employment with my firm on the condition he leave behind his questionable habits. All went well for several months until he told me one day that I should take his name off the wages journal as he was receiving unemployment benefits. I replied that was impossible. I had the respect of all the working staff and he had broken his word. I told him that he should tell the unemployment authorities what had happened. From that moment, his world and my world were both about to change. 'If you don't do this thing, I will not let you see my sister,' he retorted. Just like that, with a snap of his fingers he said, 'You will never see her again.' His employment was terminated, and I hoped to goodness I would never see him again.

That night I received a phone call from my girlfriend saying that although she was not allowed to see me, her feelings had not changed. She asked if I still felt the same way about her. Of course, I did, and we agreed that sooner or later we would see one another.

I needed space to think this latest incident over. I planned to go to the Kurrajong Health Farm situated in the Blue Mountains. I had discovered the place several years earlier and it was just the spot to go if one was depressed, overweight or stressed.

It was 22 November 1989, at 5.30pm. Whilst driving down Banna Avenue on my way to the farm, I happened to glance over to my right. Not far from the Westpac Bank was my girlfriend, Jacqui, her toddler son, Walter, and her mother. My girlfriend also noticed me and waved, indicating for

me to come over, so this I did, distancing the car from her mother. Jacqui immediately walked over to the car, asking where I was going.

'Away, far away, why don't you come with me?' I asked her.

My girlfriend said she would. If I would accept her son as mine, she would elope with me.

'Why not?' I said. It was not her fault. As far as I was concerned, she did her duty as a wife, so why mess with a little child's life? Also, he was a likeable little tot. Then came the task of coaxing little Walter away from my wife's mother. He was being held firmly. Jacqui waved her son to come to her, whereupon he broke away from his grandmother's grasp and ran to his mother. When he arrived, my girlfriend quickly put him in the back seat of the two-door *Tarago* and got into the car herself. Her mother, realising what was happening, chased after us.

With the car door still open, we took off with my future mother-in-law in pursuit, screaming at us to come back. This incident all happened on Banna Avenue.

It was our intention to stay at my mother's place, as we both knew they would come after us. Preparing myself for the affray that was about to happen, I went to change into my shorts. I was down to my underpants when Jacqui's mother came storming through the backdoor. Seeing me only in my underpants put her in shock. She just looked. I too was surprised how quickly she arrived at our house.

I took advantage. Whilst she demanded I give her back her daughter and grandson, I pushed her out of my mother's house. At that stage, her son had not arrived. I quickly locked the door as well and every window in the house. She appeared as if she was going to knock the door down. I watched through the window adjacent to the road, and saw her son enter my mother's property. Opening the window to stop him, I destroyed the mosquito protector. As I went to jump out of the window, my terrified girlfriend leapt on my back, pleading with me not to go as her brother would more than likely kill me.

Her little son was crying and coughing, whilst my dear mother could only look on in bewilderment, saying, 'What's happening, what's going on?' The banging on the back door and the screaming had reached a crescendo. There wasn't much I could do. My girlfriend's toddler had life-threatening asthma, my mother was elderly, and Jacqui would not get off my back. I ushered my mother and Walter into the bathroom and, with Jacqui still on my back, I called the police. By now, the neighbours had gathered as the banging on the door continued. I was preparing for the door to smash. This went on for a while, until they left. Shortly after, the police arrived. My future wife was a mess. She kept passing out, she had been very afraid of her brother. I preferred not to lay charges.

My girlfriend was afraid her brother would come back, so that night we decided we would all spend the night in a Narrandera Motel. Jacqui was still unwell and continued to throw up in the motel. Eventually, when she was better, she told me and my mother the true story of her life. She told us her mother was not her real mother: she was her aunt. Her brother was really her cousin. Life was hard in South America, with Jacqui's father leaving her mother when she was pregnant with her.

Her mother worked several jobs to keep her children, but, with the disappearance of her husband, she could not cope and Jacqui was put in an orphanage. After six weeks, Jacqui was taken out by her mother's sister and brought up as her own daughter. Jacqui would see her mother often as she was growing up but was told her new mother was her aunt and that now she also had a new brother as well as two sisters. Upon learning this, I thought her aunt had made a wonderful gesture because she had shown compassion in taking Jacqui out of the orphanage. Her aunt had brought her up strictly. She went to church and was not allowed to talk to boys, as I heard from the South American community in Griffith.

However, it was time for change and Jacqui's new mother

and new brother migrated to Australia, leaving Jacqui in the care of her grandmother and able to see her biological mother and sisters. My wife-to-be was about 16 years old at the time. (So as not to confuse the reader, I will change dialogue here by calling her de-facto mother and brother as her aunt and cousin.) At the age of 17, Jacqui's cousin paged her to come to Australia. That was on 24 September 1984.

That same year my mother finished work at Griffith Base Hospital. I remember whilst Jacqui's cousin was bagging onions in a packing shed, he told me he was bringing his sister out from South America. I thought little of it at the time, as she was far too young. However, here I was six years later with a pretty lass who had been married, separated and left with a child, all within 14 months.

To continue my story, we went back to my mother's place the following day. The news had spread among the South American community, with some coming over to my mother's house offering help. That was something we could do with, as my girlfriend was left only with the clothes on her back. It was the same with her son. Since Jacqui had been banished by her cousin and her son needed medical treatment for his asthma, we contacted the police. However, her street-wise cousin knew the ropes and only the medicine Ventolin and Becotide, along with the machine and puffer were returned. They would not give her back her clothing, toiletries and furniture; they wouldn't give her back anything. *Rather cruel*, I thought. *Must be how the South Americans do it over there.*

This could not go on. We purchased a few clothes in town

to get by, but we needed to get Jacqui's clothes and furniture out. To go through the courts would take too long, as her wily cousin could always stall proceedings.

We stayed at mother's for about four weeks, then decided to move into a flat. We would go to Jacqui's aunt and cousin's house and take back what belonged to her. This was not going to be that difficult as my girlfriend had the key to the house. There was a week to go before the rent had to be paid. Up to that point, the rent was paid by Jacqui. We knew where her cousin and aunt worked, in a packing shed about 30 kilometres away. With our pickup truck, we removed Jacqui's clothes and furniture and whatever else belonged to her. To make sure everything was all right, I would ring the farmer enquiring if they were still there. The farmer always replied, 'No, no, keep robbing, everything's alright, they are still here.' I couldn't help but laugh at the farmer's humour.

Several friendly South Americans helped us. The furniture was safely displayed in our flat, but when Jacqui's cousin and aunt arrived home there was bedlam. Jacqui's cousin arrived to find his mother's pot plant had been broken. Jacqui's relatives called the police, and being that we were the number one suspects, the police called around to our flat. They were invited in for a coffee. They smiled and said, 'We know you did not pinch what is obviously yours, or you'd have made an attempt to hide these things.' The police were satisfied that the clothes, furniture and toiletries were my girlfriend's, and they left.

The only other incident was that we received a summons to appear in court. Among other things, the broken pot plant was included. My girlfriend and I appeared, the other party did not. Things were starting to calm down. Apart from predictions that my girlfriend Jacqui would last two weeks with me, and at the most three months, we were left alone.

We had fun times at the flat. I had about 20 packets of talcum powder at my mother's home. Most of these I brought to the flat, where in fun we would tip them over our heads and on the bed with little Walter joining in. Even cleaning up the mess was fun. The damper on our six months happy stay at the flat was little Walter's life-threatening asthma. Every two hours throughout the night, he would be on his Ventolin and Becotide with the puffer and machine. At the age of two, Walter was pronounced dead by his doctor. He received the last rites by the parish priest, Father Rafe Beltrame.

Many a time Walter would say, 'Now I die,' with his face all blue and his stomach stuck inside his ribs. His mother would go to his school, Saint Mary's, at Yoogali, twice a day to administer medicine with the puffer. Through all this, Walter survived to become a strong, handsome young man, happy in his employment.

Around 20 June 1990, we moved into our new home of 21 Hudson Street, next door to my mother's house where she resided at 23 Hudson Street. This was only made possible by mother's great love for her son. When initially my mother told me, I doubted it could be done. I had $20,000 in the bank and a bad record with the finance companies. The house had practically been sold to other people. However, my mother said, 'Leave it to me, son.' With her amazing persuasive powers, she talked her neighbour and good friend into selling the house to me. Our neighbour said to us it was only for the great respect they had for my mother that they allowed the house to be sold to us at such a late stage.

My mother gave me $60,000 and told me to pay it back when I could. How did my mother come by this money, when during her vegetable and fruit picking days she always struggled? It was the same when she grew vegetables on that five-acre farm block of 737 Yenda. Once, when growing vegetables, she received a tuppence halfpenny stamp as payment; another time she received a bill for the produce that had been sent. Because of the hot weather, the vegetables would often arrive damaged and be condemned. They sometimes took 24 hours to arrive at the markets by train. However, Mum would say to me, 'Look after the pennies, son, and the shillings will take care of themselves.' In her case, they certainly did. With those 26 years at the hospital in permanent work, my mother must have certainly saved the pennies, shillings and the pounds. I was forever grateful, as I was now able to look after my wife, child and beloved mother.

Things continued to be good except for my girlfriend's passport, which she could not find. When she took her clothes and furniture back, the South Americans told us that her cousin had burned her passport in anger. However, that could never be proven. It made things difficult because if we did not find her permanent residency status, my wife-to-be could have been deported for overstaying her visa. A visit to a friendly Federal MP cleared the way for us to go to the South American Embassy in Sydney, where it was revealed my girlfriend was a permanent resident of Australia.

By now, my girlfriend was pregnant. She presented me with another little Australian, who came into the world on 19 August 1990. I was extremely happy: my first child, a baby boy, at 53 years old! What's more, my mother had become a grandmother for the first time after such a long wait. Young Paul was named after my father, Paul Lorenzo Guerra. We baptised him in the Catholic Church, but getting ourselves married within the church was not so easy. In fact, it was extremely difficult. We continued to go to church and receive the sacraments, much to the frustration of the parish priest. The Catholic Church frowns on divorce. It looked as if we were to be forever living in sin. I took my stand; if we couldn't marry within my Catholic faith, then we would always remain as de facto.

Child after child came along, with Jacqui presenting me with another son plus three daughters. With Walter, we have three sons and three daughters. All were baptised as Catholics. After 10 years the parish priest obtained permission from Rome and my wife's first marriage was annulled. For obvious reasons, known only to the church, I was finally to be married within my Catholic faith at the Scalabrini Chapel in Yoogali.

For me, and especially for my mother, it was an emotional event. My mother had finally succeeded in watching her son become married. My mother's prediction so many years ago that my wife-to-be had not yet been born and also that she would come from the other side of the world became eerily true.

My mother had suffered the heartbreak of not seeing her son married because of my wild ways, or because I did not want to, or perhaps because of our family stigma with insanity. Now, her prayers at last were to be answered. My wife too was extremely happy, as she had been fretting for a long time at not being able to become married within our faith. Justice had been done in God's eyes, the Vatican and the Wagga Diocese.

A lot of credit should be given to the parish priest at Griffith. He was absolutely magnificent; he knew both our histories from the moments we were born. Destiny is a strange thing, isn't it, in our case anyway. No matter how much we try to make something happen, if it is not meant to be, it is not meant to be.

It could be said we saved each other. My wife was deprived

of a father who abandoned her; I lost my father to a terrible fate. We both wanted lots of children and we both wanted to stay married to each other, no matter what.

In my time of adversity, I lost everything except my wife and children. Even the house my mother bought for me may be lost to the banks. We will wait and see.

My mother's house is now an estate and will pass on to our children when they reach the appropriate age.

The 35 years I lasted in road transport and the fruit and vegetable freight forwarding business had to be the roughest and toughest challenges of my business life. I am proud of what was achieved. I may have gone to the extreme in my attempts to please the growers and the fruit agents, but is that not what this business of cut-throat is all about: to please the customer and keep his patronage?

I have lost the fair-weather friends; they are gone forever. I only recognise them when I see them and look the other way. I have lost some growers' patronage. Whilst it is not my business anymore, it was important they stayed loyal to the new company.

Set up by the administrator, one person, I think he was Lebanese, said to me, 'You try to become a millionaire, but you fail. Why for you buy all them trucks?'

That was a fair comment. I suppose some people were happy to see a tall poppy fall over. It was not the first time this comment was said to me. The former Guerra Transport business appears to be going well under the new owners, with some of the staff being at the forefront of what is still a great business.

This story was told to commemorate the strength and tenacity shown by my mother during those early Depression years, when life was hard for everybody. With her determination not to give up, she raised a strong son and looked after her own mother for 25 years. She showed her son there was no mental illness within our family; it was just a terrible mistake. Because of apathy and ignorance, our family and relatives were tainted with a stigma of insanity that still remains with us today. I also wrote this story to assist people suffering from depression. When my mother would sometimes become down, in the blues, or depressed, she would turn to God and pray. Her medicine would be the thought of who would look after her son and her mother if she gave up?

People today have many alternatives if they become depressed, mentally ill, schizophrenic or A.D.H.D. With the understanding of medicine, much can be done, such as programs to exercise the brain and counselling.

It is said 25 percent of the community suffers from different types of mental illness, but because of modern medicine and other strategies, people can lead ordinary lives. Some doctors and psychologists say that one out of two within the community will suffer some form of mental illness in their lifetime.

Spare a thought for my grandfather, who had none of the advantages mentioned except promises from his new sons-in-law to assist him once he gave his blessing and allowed them to marry his daughters. It has been said by some relatives (and also my late mother) that Don Moretto who married grandfather's 15-year-old daughter, Maria Rosa, promised he would stay for six months and live on farm block 737 with his young bride, to help grandfather plant vegetables to bring in much needed funds.

That promise was not kept. Mr Moretto, once married, moved to Bilbul with his wife and lived happily ever after. My grandfather was not able to get along with his son, Giuseppe, who lived on his farm in Beelbangera. He was mocked by some of the townspeople of Yenda, probably because he was not able to speak English. The lump on the side of his jaw and seeing another one of his daughters leave without a husband could have been what caused my grandfather to beat his slow-thinking son, Natale. Upon this, his wife left him and went to live with her eldest daughter, Anna, in Hanwood. A heartbroken grandfather sought refuge in a mental hospital, where he stayed until taken out 10 years later by my mother and her youngest sister.

It is thought the Agostino family was the first to move to Yenda from the southern parts of Calabria. They purchased farm block 737 in July 1935. Only a handful of Calabrian families have preferred to live in Yenda. All have left except for perhaps one family.

How different it is today, with a huge Calabrian population living in Griffith, Leeton, Yanco, Wamoon and the outer townships of Tharbogang, Hanwood, Yoogali, Beelbangera and Bilbul. Today, the Calabrese are one of the kindest, most warm-hearted people there are in Griffith and district, though quick to come up with their fists if they are insulted or provoked. Proof of their kindness is that when one of their daughters or sons marry, practically all the *paisani* are invited. It is not uncommon to have 1000 or more people invited to celebrate their children's weddings. They have assimilated well and are into almost all sports within the district. It also cannot be ignored that Aussies with Calabrese and Sicilian surnames do a tremendous amount of charity work, helping the underprivileged, as taught to them by their forefathers.

So, it is with the other half of me. The Northern Italian blood flowing through my veins wants to know why a strong young man was taken away so cruelly, put in a mental asylum and virtually forgotten. Why was more not done in those critical months, even early years? We still talk about the tragedy with my Northern Italian cousins from across the border in Victoria and we always will.

The last of my father's brothers passed away recently on the 13 February 2006 at the age of 98. Giuseppe Guerra was born on the 9 March 1908. It does appear longevity is on the Guerra side. Racked with pain, tuberculosis finally took my father at the age of 72. He died alone at Ryde Psychiatric

Hospital. I couldn't bear to see him like that, it was too much. After the last time I saw my father in 1972, I was afraid I too might lose my mind.

My mother and I arranged to have dad brought to Griffith. He was buried in 1977 in the old Catholic cemetery. It was pleasing to see a large group of people attending my father's funeral. It was my mother's wish that her son Raymond was buried with dad too, and when it was her time, she should also be buried with her beloved husband and son.

As to my comments earlier in this book regarding my father's friends from Northern Italy abandoning him in his time of need; although I have forgiven them, my thoughts are the same. However, there was not a large Italian presence living in Griffith in the 1930s. The half a dozen or so really good friends of my father took the easy way out, by saying, 'Once they go like that, put them away, leave them alone and forget about them.' This was probably through fear, ignorance or because of Italy being plunged into a war against Australia.

Wogs

A story told to me recently by a small business woman in Griffith goes like this: Where would we be without you *wogs*. Us Aussies would probably starve. Your wineries alone provide over 1000 jobs within Griffith and Yenda.

That was a fair comment, I thought, and thinking about it, the big vegetable, onion and rock melon growers would probably provide half that amount, as would the packing sheds and citrus farms when in season. Then there are the business houses; half the shops seem to be owned by us *wogs*, patronised by us Aussies, bringing to mind the eternal battle of who I am: my wife speaks English, picking it up from myself and our children, our children can't speak Italian or South American and we mostly speak English at our house. However, my Aussie friends mention the word *wog* quite freely in front of me. They don't mean to offend; it's just the way it is. It rankles a bit, probably because of the way I grew up. It's just as bad for me with the Italians, especially the Italians from Southern Italy who sometimes refer to Aussies as *ingrise,* or *gringos,* or *kangaroo klunks.* This came from the people of my era mostly when I was in business several years ago. I have made many Aussie friends, some of whom I would be prepared to risk my life for. It does upset me a bit. Our children all have Aussie and multi-cultural friends with no hint of racism or anything. I thank God.

So, who am I?

An Aussie, a *woggie,* or a *wossie?*

An Aussie, of course, only sometimes I become a *wossie*; that is when I'm not really accepted as an Aussie or a *woggie.*

The wheel turns

This has nothing to do with the splendid contributions Northern Italians have made to the community of Griffith. It is mindboggling to see both Northern and Southern Italians entering the field of medicine as doctors, and getting jobs as lawyers, accountants, real estate agents, airline pilots, nurses, policemen, engineers; the list goes on.

In sport, names come up such as Bertoldo, Rossetto and Moraschi, representing their state of New South Wales and Riverina in rugby league. In soccer, it is mostly Aussies with Italian names.

In tennis, rugby union, boxing, Aussie rules, cricket, touch football and decathlon events such as the triathlon, they have excelled and done their country proud. How different it is now to the 1930s, 1940s and 1950s, when to be Italian and excel was deemed not politically correct.

In local government, we have one man who reached the highest honour, when John Dal Broi became Lord Mayor of Griffith. It doesn't stop there. On a state level, we have The Honourable Tony Catanzariti, a member of the Labor Party Legislative Assembly representing his state of NSW. Keeping him honest is the National Party Member for Murrumbidgee, Adrian Piccoli, a successful solicitor before he followed his calling. Both these outstanding citizens were born and bred in Griffith to migrant families.

It gets better, with Frank Sartor, son of a struggling migrant farmer from Yenda, becoming Mayor in the City of Sydney for some years. Frank was born and raised in Yenda. Frank Sartor was to reach further horizons when he became State Labor Minister for Energy. He appears to come from a determined and talented family. One of his sisters studied to become a barrister, another sister married an American sailor, whilst his brother became a large rock melon grower. It is not certain what his other brother and sister are doing.

Let us also look at the power base of Labor politics in NSW, with the top of the crop being the Premier of NSW, Morris Iemma, son of Calabrian migrants who came from the township of Gioiosa Ionica. This is the same town as my mother, grandmother, grandfather and also my mother's brothers and sisters were born. He is in good company, with the aforementioned Frank Sartor, John Della Bosca, Sandra Nori and Joe Tripodi, all in high echelons of power within the Labor movement (as of Sunday, 30 April 2006).

In sport, on a national scale in rugby union, we have John Earlies and the goose-stepping David Campese, in rugby league there is Minichello, and in Aussie rules there is Barassi, La Rocca, Guerra and many others. Boxing's Mattiolli, Gattellari and Ferrerri have all represented their country, Australia, at the highest level. In soccer, several Aussies with Italian names are in the World Cup side. How proud they must have made their parents. Equally as pleased in sports-mad Australia are we, as Aussies, who love our sport so much it has helped to make us among the best sporting nations in the world.

How different it is today to yesteryear! In 1926, the newspaper *Smith's Weekly* printed that Italians were a "dirty dago pest", yet our forefathers rose above the bigotry, jealousy and misunderstanding to win over a once hostile press. Even up to the mid-fifties, it was practically taboo for an Italian to marry an Australian girl. Having a conversation with a friend, I was told he was only the second Italian to marry an Australian at Yenda in that era (1955-56). Time is a great healer. A decade later, it was noticeable more

Italians (or rather, more Aussies) were marrying Australian girls. Today, up to 50 percent of true-blue Aussies with Italian names are marrying Australian girls in Griffith. What a wonderful city we have grown into, with hardly any unemployment and some racist bias towards one another is still there, but it has gone underground. We Australians in Griffith and Yenda are bonding and working together to make our cities even greater.

Before my time is up, it is my wish to see Yenda become a sprawling metropolis rivalling Griffith. I am sure my mother, and those hundreds of pioneers who fought and died on the battlefields of the Murrumbidgee Irrigation Area, trying to defeat a sometimes unruly, windswept, hot and dusty land with no Centrelink or pension payments to assist them, can smile in satisfaction knowing they have left a legacy for their sons and grandsons, daughters and granddaughters to carry on.

The wheel turns

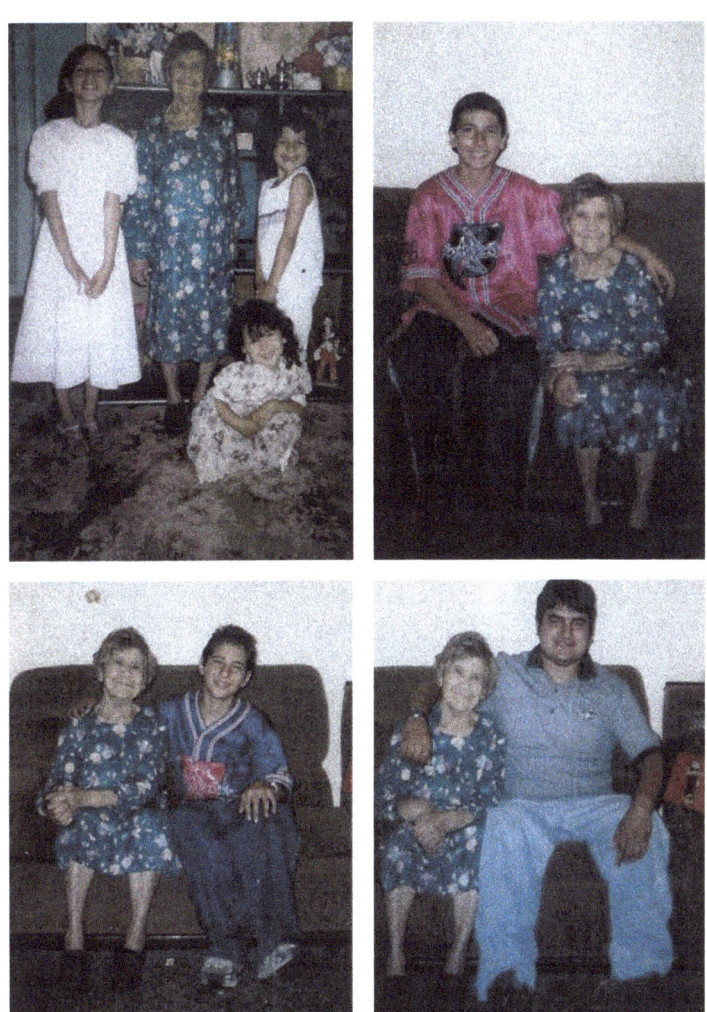

In June 1999 the *Area News* wrote a two-and-a-half-page tribute to my mother.

After the passing of my mother, I added my brother's baby booties to the newspaper cutting of her photos, as they were the only possessions she had to remind her of the baby son she had lost.

www.ingramcontent.com/pod-product-compliance
Lightning Source LLC
Chambersburg PA
CBHW040106120526
44588CB00039B/2753